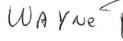

Two Decades and Counting

The Streak

The Wins

The Hawkeyes

Thru the Eyes of Roy Marble

Brian D. Meeks

Two Decades and Counting

The Streak, The Wins, The Hawkeyes: Thru the Eyes of Roy
Marble

All Rights Reserved
Published by
Brian D. Meeks
111 W Kohl
Box 71
Martelle, IA 51305
http://ExtremelyAverage.com
Brian@ExtremelyAverage.com

ISBN-13: 978-0-9851046-0-3

Table of Contents

29. Ohio State: Iowa Record (22–3)
30. Indiana: Iowa Record (23–3)
31. Michigan State: Iowa Record (23–4)
32. Michigan: Iowa Record (24–4)
33. Northwestern: Iowa Record (25–4)
34. Wisconsin: Iowa Record (26–4)
35. NCAA Tournament: Selection Sunday
36. Santa Clara: Iowa Record (27-4)
37. UTEP: Iowa Record (28-4) <Not included yet
38. Oklahoma: Iowa Record (29-4)
39. UNLV: Iowa Record (30-4)
40. 2012–Spring

A young boy sits on the edge of his bed. He holds it in his right hand, the movements are measured; the weight is familiar. Just to be sure, he crosses it over to his left hand, and it is undeniably perfect. There is one more test, at least, which is allowed in the house. A few moments of looking at the seams, reading the words "Official NBA," and then with the slightest toss, he brings both hands together, violently smacking the ball. The sound is unmistakable, if not indescribable.

It is that singular note that sparks the dream. One thinks of dreams as images flashing through the mind, but it is the sounds that bore deep into the soul. It is sneakers on blacktop, then hard wood. It is the sound of chain, then cord. It is the cheers of teammates, then crowds. It is a symphony when playing in the mind of a boy in Flint, Michigan. It is the sirens' call.

One

The sound of the shoes is unmistakable. It is of heavy feet on hard wood and the pounding of the ball being moved up the court. Summer in North Liberty, Iowa, means basketball. People pack the gym to watch present, future, and current college players doing what they love. The passes are crisp and, though it is a summer league, the games are more about the team than the individuals. These kids have grown up in gyms like this one, with coaches and tournaments, just to gain that one extra step. The names on the jerseys look familiar. There is a Marble and a Stokes running the floor and, to watch, one would think time had stood still these past twenty-five years.

Anthony Hubbard, a current Hawkeye, drives the lane, gets hacked, and deftly guides a left-handed shot off the board. He converts the three-point play. They are down by one, with 3 minutes left in the first half. To look at it, one would think it was the NCAA tournament: guys diving for rebounds, making steals, and pushing themselves as they are accustomed to doing. The gym continues to swell with people trying to get a glimpse.

Halftime is considerably more informal than it is at Carver Hawkeye Arena. The players talk with friends and family in the stands. A few rest on the bench while the coaches mingle with the referees. The clock falls below a minute, and people start to take their seats. The second half of the first game is about to begin. The score is 50–52.

People talk about the coming Hawkeye season with summer optimism when it seems all things are possible. Roy Marble sits behind the basket, watching his son as a father, a coach, a fan. Twenty-five years ago, he was playing in the First Prime Time League. He felt good back then, with the same optimism, but nobody knew what was about to happen. Not even Roy.

Two

1986

Anchorage is a long way from Flint, Michigan, he thought to himself, as he got off the charter plane. It would be nice to get the season started, but damn it was cold. The wind was brutal and stinging, but soon they were inside, and his mind turned back to the games to come.

Run D.M.C. was dominating the hip-hop scene and had crossed over to become the first group from this genre nominated for a Grammy Award. Their King of Rock album ran through Roy's headphones and into the depth of his soul. Music lifted him up to places he was unaware even existed. The beat made it easy to push, to work, to reach for greatness.

The "Great Alaska Shootout" was an annual tournament in which the Hawkeyes would face three quality opponents, and it was an honor to be invited. The tournament was a great way to begin a season as long as you came away with two wins. Seven teams were always invited to the home of Alaska-Anchorage. It was a solid collection of talent, with the likes of Texas, NC State, Northeastern, Louisville, Utah State, Washington, and the University of Iowa, who would play the host team in the first game of the tournament.

The television was on in the room. Roy sat on the edge of the bed, checking out ESPN but mostly just pushing out the noise. He didn't ever take for granted the opportunity that basketball had given him. A lifetime love affair with the game had taught him enough to be asked to represent the University of Iowa—as a player and as a person. The school would provide a place where he could further his education, both on and off the court, and as the highlights flashed across the screen, he thought about the off-court lessons.

Earning the right to play Division I sports was an accomplishment in and of itself. When one arrived on campus, there were dozens of paths laid out before a young man or woman. There were new experiences and challenges every single day. Roy thought about all of the people he had met over the past year in Iowa City. When he first set foot on campus, it seemed that every day there were dozens of new people coming into his life. When you were in the new basketball class, people were naturally interested in getting to know you. They were friendly and engaging. They wanted to be in your circle, and as a young man out of Flint, it was a daily deluge of newness for Roy, which could make seeing the correct path a challenge.

Roy knew where he wanted the path to lead. It was a very exclusive community called the National Basketball Association, and he had dreamed of that day since he started to have people tell him he had "game." What he had learned after a year in college was that there wasn't just one path to the NBA. There were several, all with similar basketball requirements, but some with other challenges. Some athletes decided that everything unrelated to their sport was a distraction that wouldn't help them achieve their goals. Roy saw things differently. He thought about the woman who showed him the value of using all that the University had to offer. She had sold him on the classes, the studying, and the logic of exercising his brain more than just for the game of basketball. The better you were at thinking, she said, the better you would be at thinking on the court.

A knock at the door and one of the coaches yelled, "Twenty minutes!" and moved on down the hall.

Lou Kelly didn't win him over right away, however. She was his rhetoric professor, and Fred Mims had once told Roy, "Don't come running to me complaining about Lou Kelly. If you don't do what she says, you won't play." It was a powerful motivator, and she eventually won Roy over. She would demand that he work on his writing or speaking, and he would ask why? She would tell him, and he would shrug. No matter how many different arguments he threw up, she would swat them all into the bleachers. They had this same conversation many times, but like a relentless power forward, she kept driving her point home. Roy was powerless against her full-court press. He loved her for it.

It was a struggle between the comfort zone of what was known and the difficulty in reaching for something unfamiliar. Thousands of athletes across the country deal with this when they reach college for the first time. At home, they are big fish in little ponds. They have their family, their friends, the comfort of their favorite places to hang out. But suddenly, in one day, it all seems to vanish. It can be hard, and those who succeed figure out how to choose their paths and push the uncomfortable feeling of the newness aside. They embrace the change, the newness, and the excitement of what lies ahead.

It wasn't until he started to have success in the classroom and realized that he could be a winner there, too, that he came around to Lou Kelly's way of thinking. The better he got at studying, the easier he found that it added to his basketball knowledge. Roy realized that knowing how to learn makes the task much easier. He could understand tendencies of his opponents quicker. This gave him an edge. Every new team would approach the game differently, and the quicker he could adapt, the more unstoppable he would become.

When Roy decided his path included class work, he knew he was choosing a more difficult route, but he also knew that the life it led to was a better one.

ESPN continued on in the background while Roy checked his bag. Roy had a routine, and once it began, his brain switched into game mode. He was no longer thinking about Anchorage, the cold, the miles between him and Flint, or even a dedicated teacher. He was thinking about the lessons his new coach, Dr. Tom Davis, had taught him. He was thinking about his opponent. He was thinking about winning.

Three

The 1986 season saw a new captain at the helm of the Iowa Hawkeye's ship. Dr. Tom Davis, who knew a thing or two about choosing a path that included education, came to Iowa from Stanford. Before his four years at Stanford, he had been the head coach at Boston College where he had led the Eagles to an Elite 8 appearance in the '81 –'82 season. In college, Davis was the point guard at the University of Wisconsin-Platteville. After college, he had several coaching gigs before landing an assistant coaching position at the University of Maryland in 1967 under Frank Fellows. While he was assistant coach, Tom Davis completed his doctorate and earned the moniker Dr. Tom.

As a student of the game, Davis had developed a strategy of using a greater depth of his roster. He believed in teaching the young men to play hard, to keep moving, and to wear the other team out. His frequent substitutions and fast tempo made for an exciting brand of basketball. He was a great teacher, and Roy loved playing for him.

Dr. Tom earned Roy's respect, and it wasn't a layup either. His predecessor, George Raveling, had not only recruited Roy, he had brought in two other Michigan players, Bill Jones and B.J. Armstrong. Coach Raveling knew how to recruit and also won over Ed Horton, Kevin Gamble, Gerry Wright, and Les Jepsen. It was hard on Roy when Coach Raveling left, and there was even a moment when he considered following him to USC. But in the end, Iowa City had become his basketball home. Roy loved the town and the people, and the new coach was a good one.

That first night, so many miles from Iowa City, Roy saw the familiar Black and Gold in the stands. Did they come for the games, or did they live there? Hawkeye fans were everywhere. After long hours, hard work, and the music in his mind, his sophomore season was about to begin. Roy was ready. All the Hawks were as well.

On the hardwood floors, on any given night, the best team wins 100 percent of the time. The fun is finding out who will be the best team on any given night. The Iowa Hawkeyes, from the powerhouse Big Ten conference, would have been the easy team to pick. The Hawkeyes had a preseason ranking of number ten in the country. They would have been expected to win the first game of the Great Alaska Shootout. The fans sitting at the Sports Column, in Iowa City, would have been expecting them to win big.

This is the dilemma faced by every coach—to instill a sense of confidence without creating a feeling of cockiness. It is less difficult to motivate a team on their first game. The long practices, running, conditioning, and anticipation make the guys eager to finally start playing. Of course, the young men of the University of Alaska-Anchorage had been working just as hard, and this was their tournament. They also had four games under their belts and were 4–0.

The Sullivan Arena was packed with 4,369 fans, all excited to see the tournament get underway, and they weren't disappointed. The record for scoring in a single game was matched, but not by a member of the highly touted Iowa squad. The line read 14 for 30 from the field, 6 for 7 from the line, for a total of 37 points, by number 21, Jessie Jackson of UAA.

The first half was an exciting one, and the Hawkeyes went into the break with a slim three-point lead. At 47–44, the UAA Seawolves were a single shot from tying up the game. Inside the Sports Column more beers were being ordered while the crowd of coaches debated the play. There was excitement and nervousness. The optimists talked about the great plays of their opponent and gave credit to the men in Black and Gold for holding them off. The pessimists were writing off the whole season and quite sure that the apocalypse was at hand. This is the nature of being a fan.

Early in the second half, the Seawolves took the lead. The Hawkeyes stepped up their defense and held the UAA scoreless for 4 minutes. Brad Lohaus, a seven-footer who shoots like a guard, scored 11 points in the second half, finishing with 15. Facing an opponent who was almost best, the Hawkeyes won as a team. They spread the points around and, when the clock ran down to zero, were ahead 91–81. Roy Marble had 18; BJ Armstrong added 16, including 8-of-8 from the free throw line;

Horton had 12; and everyone played tough defense in stopping the Seawolves. That is how the best team won, but just barely. Still, when they went to sleep that night, Dr. Tom Davis's players had a newfound respect for the Seawolves and their star, J.J. The folks at the Sports Column were satisfied with the outcome and celebrated with a rousing "In Heaven There Is No Beer." Even the pessimists.

Day one ended with even more excitement: N.C State 69–Texas 66, Northeastern 88–Louisville 84 OT, and Utah State 81–Washington 72. And that is why it isn't called the Average Alaska Shootout.

Four

2011–Fall

It is a powerful word, "team." In the early years, during second or third grade, we are assigned to a team in gym class. Young feet begrudgingly run up and down the gymnasium floor, praying for the madness to end. A few love it. They get a taste for competition, and the sweetness of victory is greater than the bitterness of defeat. Nobody likes to lose, and those who turn to a life of competition like it less than most, but it doesn't stop them. That is what makes a champion—the love of the game, more than the loathing of the pain.

It is but a few who know what it is like to be chosen by a university. By the time high school ends, most are done with team sports. It is on to school or work, starting a family, and turning their competitive juices towards fandom. It may not be as fun as playing, but cheering is a close second. The fastest, strongest, and hardest workers get asked to compete at the college level and often are rewarded with scholarships. The first-year players learn from the older ones, and strangers become teammates. Over time, they become friends. Success and winning come not only from having talent, but also from the bond between the players. If one truly cares about his teammates, he will find ways to push beyond what he thought was possible. When those bonds form, they last for life.

Roy's high school coach, Moses Lacy, who went 27–0 and won the state title in 1985 for Flint's "Buc-Town" Beecher High School, told Roy once, "In order to be a great player, you must be a great teammate first."

Roy's phone rings and he checks the number, "Yo, Mike Mo."

Michael Morgan, an assistant coach with the University of Iowa Women's basketball team for the last seven years, was part of the 1986 team. He received the most "Most Dedicated Player Award" that year and made the most of his college years getting a bachelors degree in communications studies. As they talk, first about family and kids, then about basketball, Morgan says something and Roy laughs.

"Mike, you remember the trip to China?"

"You aren't still laughing about that," he says.

The team was touring and, on a day off, got to do some sightseeing. You can't go to China without seeing the Great Wall, so that was high on the list of places the team wanted to see. While taking photos, Michael slipped and broke the lens on his camera. Michael wasn't injured, so it seemed fine to give him a hard time about it. It would have probably been forgotten had it not been for Kent Hill's comment on the flight home, "Mike Mo fell off the Great Wall of China," he said, recounting the highlights of their trip. Everyone laughed, and it became one of those stories that guys tell over and over again, and, for a moment, recapture those wonderful days of college.

They talk a while longer. Roy mentions the Alaska shootout, and they both agree it was a great way to start the season. One last check to ask Michael if there are any new stories to pass along, and then he hangs up. To tell the old stories again keeps them alive and makes it a special time.

Roy remembers Michael as a friend and a teammate, but mainly he remembers how hard Mike Mo would push him in practice. It is one thing to work as hard as you think you can, but another to have someone you trust saying you can go harder. When Michael got minutes and Roy was on the bench, there wasn't anyone cheering him on louder. Michael made Roy a better player, and to this day he is thankful.

Five

A woman wearing a NC State sweatshirt leapt to her feet, and it caught Roy's eye. The Wolfpack ran onto the floor confidently as their coach followed behind. He was Jimmy "V," the legendary coach, who took the '82–'83 team all the way to the NCAA finals and faced Houston. Roy remembered watching the game and the amazing dunk. Houston was heavily favored because of its center, Hakeem Olajuwon. With the score tied at 52, a rainbow shot from Dereck Whittenburg missed the mark, but Lorenzo Charles was right there and slammed it home. Jim Valvano's Wolfpack won the national championship. The image of him running around the floor, showing the pure exuberance that only sports can provide, is one that will never be forgotten by anyone who has seen that final moment.

Roy grabbed a ball as it swished through the hoop and lightly jogged to fifteen feet from the rim. He needed to go through his routine but stopped and allowed himself one second of indulgence. He gave a look at the coach who was now part of basketball history. Jimmy "V" was worrying about Roy and his teammates. Alaska was a long ways from Iowa and a million miles from the couch where Roy sat in high school and watched the "Greatest Upset in NCAA History." The snapshot he took in his mind would last forever. Playing college basketball is an honor, and the experience needs to be appreciated. Doing less would be disrespectful.

Roy fired up another shot. It missed. The indulgence was over. He grabbed another ball, popped his off hand against the leather, and the click in his head brought him into game focus. Nobody tracks warm-up shots, but Roy wanted to make them all. He hated to miss—ever.

The game started out just fine. B.J. Armstrong ran the point with precision, and 11 minutes in, they led 30–20. It didn't last. Tom Davis said after the game, "We played a man (defense) early but we played it so lousy we went back to a zone." While Iowa was trying to find the key to getting stops, the Wolfpack went on a 27–14 run to finish the half.

Down by 3, 47–44, the Hawks had to struggle to keep up. With 10 minutes remaining, Bennie Bolton, Charles Shackleford, and the rest of the Wolfpack had secured a comfortable 10-point margin. They continued to press, and with 4:45 remaining, Shackleford scored. N.C State 78–Iowa 64, and it looked bad to the fans back home.

Basketball is a game of two halves, both literally and figuratively. The man-to-man defense that didn't work at first was now being played with heart and determination. A 9–0 run by the Hawkeyes had their faithful fans screaming. Hope was restored. The Iowa fans, both at the game and back home, had no idea what was coming next.

In a flurry, B.J. Armstrong hit a three-pointer, Kent Hill put it in off a rebound, Kevin Gamble drove to the basket to score, and

Brad Lohaus converted on a turnover. Iowa led 82–80. The clock was running out, and N.C. State's Shackelford tied it at 82.

Roy had played well, but the tough defense forced an error. Nobody plays flawlessly. The true measure is how one deals with mistakes. With just 39 seconds left, Roy traveled, turning over the ball. The clock read 22 seconds remaining when Kenny Drummond was sent to the line. He made them both, and N.C State led 84–82.

In North Carolina, they cheered. In Iowa, they prayed. With one second remaining, the Hawkeye's prayers were answered as Chucky Brown made an unnecessary foul on B.J. Armstrong. He would go to the line, down by 2, needing to make them both. After 39 minutes and 59 seconds of playing their hearts out, nine guys would stand on the court watching as only one had the fate of the game in his hands.

He made them both.

Overtime, well, there would be overtime, if N.C State couldn't score in the last one second. A pass to Kenny Drummond; he turned and fired. From thirty feet out, the ball hit the backboard and the rim. The buzzer sounded, and the score remained tied. He hadn't missed by much. No time to dwell on what might have been as there were 5 more minutes to play.

The overtime was as exciting as the regulation play, and when the buzzer sounded, the Hawkeyes led 90–89 and had earned the right to play in the championship game. B.J. Armstrong led all scorers with 26 points, but it is the two free throws, which will remain in the minds of the fans for a long time to come, that were crucial for the win.

Roy had poured in 19 and shook Jimmy Valvano's hand after the game. He would never forget that moment.

On March 3, 1993, Jimmy "V" gave a speech at the ESPY awards. He was being presented with the inaugural Arthur Ashe Courage and Humanitarian Award. During his speech, he announced the creation of the V Foundation, which would be dedicated to finding a cure for cancer. His speech and the motto that would drive the new foundation, "Don't Give Up ... Don't Every Give Up," sent chills throughout the sports community and will always be remembered:

"To me, there are three things we all should do every day. We should do this every day of our lives. Number one is laugh. You should laugh every day. Number two is think. You should spend some time in thought. And number three is you should have your emotions moved to tears, which could be happiness or joy. But think about it. If you laugh, you think, and you cry, that's a full day. That's a heck of a day. You do that seven days a week, you're going to have something special."

On April 28, 1993, he lost his battle with cancer.

Six

Northeastern was waiting for them. As exciting a trip as it had been for the Hawkeyes, Carl Fogel had coached his Huskies past the number two-ranked Louisville Cardinals in the first round, and then handled Utah State on Saturday for an equally thrilling ride.

Outside their respective locker rooms and the local bars where their faithful waited, few would have picked this matchup as the finals for the 1986 Great Alaska Shootout. Inside the locker rooms, Carl Fogel and Dr. Tom Davis were giving their final instructions before heading out for the opening tip.

Dr. Tom Davis isn't afraid to ask a lot of his players. They would need to respond or face a long flight home carrying the crushing defeat with them.

The Hawkeyes and Huskies were tied 6–6 after having traded baskets in the opening minutes. Roy, B.J., Brad, and the rest of the team ran hard the entire game. At half time, they led by 13, 49–36. The Huskies fought back and got within 9 early in the second half, but that would be the closest margin the rest of the night.

Roy Marble tied a career high with 29 points, matching a freshman year performance against Arkansas–Littlerock. The two strong performances leading to the finals and the 29 points earned him the MVP for the tournament. He wasn't the only star that night. Their team defense held the Huskies to 36 percent shooting, which was more than Dr. Tom Davis could have hoped for. And yet, he got more. Brad Lohaus rebounded with authority, pulling down 12 boards, and shooting 4–6 from the field. Jeff Moe had a career night as well, adding 26 points, 2 points above his high water mark, and he did it with an impressive 75 percent shooting from the field.

The Northeastern Huskies got a great game out of 6'7" Reggie Lewis, who matched Roy's output with 29 points. Reggie just didn't have the help that Roy did, and that was the difference.

The next day, the Des Moines Register's Marc Hansen ran a quote from Roy, who, when asked about the MVP, said, "I thought I could make the all-tournament team, but I never dreamed this would happen. I never dreamed we'd win by such a wide margin."

The flight back to Iowa was a breeze after the win. The Hawkeyes were 3–0, and the Tom Davis era was off to a great start.

******

Benjamin Roy Armstrong, Jr. was known simply as "B.J." or "Beejer," by his friends. Roy and B.J. met long before stepping onto the hardwood in Iowa City. They were fifteen years old. Roy was with his AAU team on a trip to Kalamazoo, and he had never seen a kid their age dribble a ball like B.J. He started to call him Lil Isiah Thomas. Later, when talking with his dad, he tried to explain how good this kid on his team was, but it was beyond words.

The excitement was evident, and Roy's father was pleased that his son had found some good kids to hang out with. Lloyd Fault, J.P Osterbaun, B.J. Armstrong, and Roy became fast friends. Roy's father, preferring that his son hang around his basketball buddies, bought him a grey Escort, so they could get around. Roy spent a lot of time in Kalamazoo.

The same AAU team got to travel to Helsinki, Finland, for two-and-a-half weeks. They had a great time and became even closer friends. At the time, Roy never thought about the future or getting recruited to play far from home.

When the recruiting trips started, B.J. headed off to Iowa City, while Roy chose to visit John Thompson at perennial power Georgetown. Roy got to stay with Patrick Ewing and Sleepy Floyd. Roy was amazed by the trip. Those guys were on TV every weekend, and he got to hang out with them. He decided to verbally commit to Georgetown because he was so impressed with how tough John Thompson was and thought he would be a great man to learn from.

On the return trip, there was a layover at the Detroit airport. It might have been fate, but he ran into his buddy B.J., who was just returning from his official visit to Iowa. These two friends sat and talked. They exchanged stories from their trips, and B.J. described the Iowa program and campus like he was describing his mother's cooking. Roy was amazed by B.J.'s enthusiasm and got excited about his upcoming trip to see Iowa City. Before they left to head their separate ways that day at the airport, Roy fired off as many questions as he could think of, and when they finally parted, he was willing to give Iowa a fair shake.

B.J. told him, "I think that's the place. I know I'm going to Iowa if you go to Iowa."

Roy said he would call as soon as he had finished his visit to Iowa.

The trip went well. Roy's mom and dad went with him. They didn't try to direct Roy to one school or the other, but waited until he asked what they thought. When asked, his parents said that they had never seen anything like Iowa. The people were genuine, hospitable, and so nice that his mother felt he would be most at home there. She was comfortable with the people who would be looking after her son, as was his dad, and Roy listened to what they had to say.

Roy was impressed, too. He made the call to his friend B.J. and they decided they would go to Iowa together. College is always better when you can go with a friend.

Seven

Winning is great. The moments after finishing on top of a tournament are amazing. Roy and his teammates celebrated with the silver plate at center court. The press snapped photos, and nobody held back their joy.

The plane left Anchorage at 4 a.m., and everyone was still riding the post game adrenaline rush. It made sleep difficult, and Roy didn't try to fight it. These were the times that he wanted to remember. Eventually, though, the adrenaline was gone, and three days of leaving it all on the court caught up with the young men on the plane. Some slept, others listened to their Walkmans, and Roy relaxed and let the weekend go.

A couple of the guys were talking about how Louisville had lost their first three games of the season, which had to be a record for a defending national champion. It made Roy think about taking teams for granted. The feeling of victory was too precious to squander with overconfidence. History was filled with great upsets and nobody ever questioned whether the vanquished favorites had let their guard down. That didn't make a good story. The Iowa Hawkeyes would now be the Goliaths, at which, the nation's Davids would be slinging their best games. Roy wasn't sure if he liked the analogy, as they were surely the good guys, but it was true nonetheless. They would be the prize for each team they met. He knew because that was how he felt playing NC State.

With success comes weight. It is added with each game, each triumph, and every step toward March. The coaches will try to tell them that the next game is all that matters, and they are right, but a streak is never silent. It whispers in your ear and tries to distract you. Each game the fans cheer a little bit louder. Clad in black and gold, they are wishing you well, but they are also asking for more with every win.

The papers write stories, but Roy doesn't read them. He never has and never will. Still, the fans do, and then there are the questions from reporters. They read each other's articles and when someone like Marc Hansen from the Des Moines Register writes, "Marble … picked up where he left off in his splendid freshman season. Because of his acrobatic style of play and his size, he is sometimes compared with Michael Jordon." It leads to other questions and comparisons. How does one answer such questions? How does one jump a bar set in the stratosphere? Roy puts it out of his mind. He knows that there is only one Michael Jordon.

The campus has been abuzz, and Roy is glad it is Wednesday. Today the season continues with a matchup against Division II Missouri-St. Louis. He is ready for the story to change.

Dr. Tom Davis knows that overconfidence can sneak up and bite a team. In discussing the relative young Hawkeyes, Rick Brown quotes Dr. Davis in his December 3 article: "Going into the season, the point guard was a big question mark for us, but B.J. stepped in and erased it. He's very calm and collected; he doesn't get rattled or upset. He accepts criticism and just listens. He nods his head and does his best. Inside maybe he's churning, but he doesn't let on to the teammates or the coaches that things bother him. That's nice for a leader to exude that kind of confidence."

Before his first game as new coach, the friendly folks in the stands at Carver Hawkeye—all 15,341 of them—sang Coach Davis a rousing "Happy Birthday." He had turned forty-eight, and it didn't look like his players were going to make it a day to remember once the game began.

It is one thing to know that overconfidence can affect play; it is another to prevent it. The Hawkeyes started the game off with 5 turnovers in the first 3½ minutes. In their previous game, the finals, they had shot 69.8 percent from the field but only managed 43.2 percent in the first half. It seemed that they were on course to ruin their head coach's 48th birthday, but then they settled down. Coach Davis said after the game, "Our offense didn't go real well, but it didn't stop us from playing defense. It was a real good win for us because we were coming off an emotional high, yet we played hard. That was very pleasing to me." The 89–64 win brought the number five-ranked Iowa Hawkeyes to 4–0 on the season.

On Friday they would face Delaware (2–0) in the Amana-Hawkeye Classic. A lot of schools host tournaments early in the season and generally invite teams they feel will not provide too much of a test. This isn't always the case, though. Iowa had finished third in their own tournament the previous year because of a first-round loss to a very good Arkansas State team. The current year's tournament also included Loyola Marymount and Washington State, who had finished fifth in the Pac-10 the previous year. If Iowa wanted to continue its unbeaten streak, it would need to continue its solid defense and improve on the lackluster shooting from Wednesday night.

******

When Roy was getting recruited, he had a lot of choices. It was a tough decision, and everyone around him had an opinion. Georgetown, under legendary coach John Thompson, went 35–3, were located in the nation's capital, and played in the Big East Conference. Michigan was an obvious choice, and a lot of people in Flint would have loved to have seen him stay near home. Marquette and DePaul were also in his top five. But it was one single moment that made Roy's decision to come to Iowa. George Raveling was an amazing recruiter. Coach Raveling had a recording of Jim Zabel, the well-known announcer, calling a game against Indiana when time was running down. Zabel said, "The ball goes to Marble and he hits the game winning shot." He played it for Roy. Hearing the sound of the crowd going crazy and his own name associated with the triumph, Roy was hooked. Iowa City would be his new home.

Eight

Delaware: Iowa Record (4–0)

Early on, the Hawkeyes had a nice little 13–0 run, but that was just the beginning. During the final 8:53 of the first half, Iowa outscored Delaware 23–0. The Bluehens were 0–10 from the field and had 4 turnovers. Iowa shot 66.7 percent from the field, while Delaware managed only 27.2 in the first half.

Senior Brad Lohaus came to play. At 5:22 remaining in the first half, he took over with a thundering dunk. Eight seconds later, he was at the free throw line making both shots and then 10 seconds after that, a steal and dunk. Over the next minute-and-a-half, he had two blocked shots and a rebound with an assist. Before the half ended, he threw down another dunk. In only 21 minutes of play, he was 6–8 from the field, 4–4 from the line, with 5 rebounds and an assist.

When Brad left the game, it was to a standing ovation of 8,340 fans in attendance. Though it was the smallest crowd in Carver Hawkeye history for a men's game, he was thankful. "My career here has been tough," he said after the game as he moved from center to forward, "but one thing I learned when I was young was to never give up. I never had any doubt I could play here, but I didn't want it to take this long. I'm just playing as hard as I can."

The game was well in hand, and coach Davis didn't squander the opportunity to go deeper into the bench. All fourteen players saw time, including Lusso, who pulled down a rebound. Lusso only saw 2 minutes, but all of the other thirteen had 8 or more minutes on the floor. There isn't anything like game experience to bring a player along, and when March arrives, depth will be important.

When asked his impressions of the game, Dr. Davis talked about the first play of the second half. Roy could have used his athleticism to take the ball to the basket on his own, but instead he dished up a pass for Brad's fourth dunk of the game. "To me that was the key play of the game," Davis said. "That was unselfish play for your so-called super star. Usually those guys want two more points for themselves. But Roy sets the tone for our whole team. He's unselfish and not out looking to polish the marble. He just plays the team game and deserves some credit for that."

******

Coaches aren't born; they are grown. The great coaches worked for the great coaches before them, who were generous with their teaching. As assistants, they watched their mentors mold young athletes, and they learned the craft. Like that of a thoroughbred horse, a coach's bloodline is checked by athletic directors when they are ready to make a hire. There are legendary bloodlines all over sports. In basketball, Dean Smith played at Kansas for Forrest "Phog" Allen, for whom "Phog Allen Field House" is named. When Dean Smith retired, he had 879 victories, and he left behind some great names to carry on. Both Larry Brown and Roy Williams are part of the Dean Smith tree, but if one looks closer, and takes a peek at the Allen tree, one sees that Allen learned his craft from James Naismith, as a player. It was James Naismith who invented basketball and planted the first seeds.

Coach Davis was helped by three assistants—Gary Close, Bruce Pearl, and Rudy Washington. Gary Close is part of the Tom Davis tree, having worked for him for four years at Stanford before joining him in Iowa City. His experience also included a five-year stint with the Phoenix Suns of the NBA. In addition, he was on Tom Davis's staff when Coach Davis took an all-star team from the Pac-Ten to tour Australia in 1985. His playing days included lettering for three years at Moorestown High School in New Jersey, where he was the captain as a senior.

Bruce Pearl was also a long-time student of the game under Davis, having been with him for nine years. He spent a lot of time on the road with recruiting responsibilities as well as learning about the vagaries of off-court duties like ticket sales, promotion, scheduling, and making travel arrangements. He played three years of high school basketball for Sharon High School and would have likely gone on to college ball had it not been for several knee injuries.

Rudy Washington, who was a holdover from the George Raveling staff, was in his second year on the Iowa staff. He had experience recruiting for Clemson, was an assistant at USC for three seasons, and worked for the Los Angeles Lakers organization. He had also been a head coach at the high school level, where he led the 1978 Verbum Dei High School team to the nation's number one ranking. He also coached the junior varsity team for his high school, Locke, where the team went an astounding 120–0.

Nine

The rankings are tough to ignore, especially when in the top ten. Of course, if one is too focused on the accolades, then one won't be ranked number five. So, the business at hand is a competent Loyola-Marymount (1–0) team who had earned their way into the finals beating Washington State 96–89.

Roy sat in the locker room going through his pre-game routine and thought about the moment. Gerry Wright had broken his hand earlier in the season, and Roy had taken it upon himself to step in and take up some of the slack, but not in the typical way. He didn't try to become a one-man force. The other men in the locker room were too talented to ignore.

The last time Iowa had played the Lions was on Dec 17, 1955, and the Hawkeyes won comfortably 84–61. Roy overheard someone mention the game from 1955 and that this was only the second time the teams had met. He couldn't imagine the significance of a game thirty years earlier, but it didn't matter if there was one or not; people's love for the game allowed for these moments. That is the beauty of sports, especially basketball, in that it isn't just the players on the court who win or lose; it is the fans who cheer their hearts out.. Who knows, maybe there is someone in the stands, right now, telling his grandchild about going to the game with his father. Perhaps that same child will talk about this game with his kids. "I had better lace them up and get ready to win," Roy thought.

The Lions coach, Paul Westhead, had a solid game plan, and it remained close during the first half and into the second. With 18 minutes remaining in the game, it was Iowa up by 3, 50–47. Coach Davis countered by going deep into his bench. He used nine players extensively and simply wore them down. Twelve players scored for Iowa. B.J. Armstrong led the Hawkeyes with 21 points and Roy added 20 more, plus pulled down 8 rebounds. The Hawkeyes out-rebounded the Lions 57–42 and closed out the game with an impressive 103–80 win. Roy picked up his second MVP trophy in a week and said afterwards, "I thought it was a tribute to me, but it was a tribute to my teammates as well."

After the game a lot of questions were directed at Roy. Since Sports Illustrated's Hank Hersch had compared him to Michael Jordan (November 19, 1986 issue), it had been the norm. Of course, wearing the iconic number 23 may have added fuel to the fire, but he could handle it. They asked about the game and then his own numbers. Roy wasn't satisfied with his level of play and answered, "I don't think I've played my best game. I still see a lot of things I could do better."

Brad Lohaus said of his teammate, "Roy is such a great player and does so many things well that if teams start slacking off and going to him, he can get rid of the ball and let other people score. And it just disrupts the whole game. You have to give a lot of credit to Roy because he performs so well under pressure."

The winning felt great. The entire Hawkeye community was cheering and supporting their efforts, and Roy sensed it was going to be a special year. That is how it was done at Iowa. Roy loved the family feel Iowa City had, and when he saw other athletes, they got along immediately. It was a great time to be wearing the black and gold. Roy's buddies Chuck Long and Larry Station were gone to the NFL, but Hayden Fry, with Mark Vlasic at the helm, had put together an 8–3 season and was getting prepared for the Holiday Bowl and San Diego State. It had been a fun season to be sure. There were rules and regulations by the NCAA about perks, but sometimes Roy would be allowed to watch a game from the press box, enjoy a hotdog, and get to cheer on his friends tearing up the gridiron.

Whenever Roy saw Coach Fry at a basketball game, he knew it meant one thing: There were some recruits in town. The moment had to be just right, but when the alleyoop play got called, and Roy finished with a thundering dunk, he would make sure to run past Hayden and make eye contact. Hayden would give him a wink, as if to say, "Well done."

Carver Hawkeye was mostly quiet now. Roy walked past C. Vivian Stringer and said, "Hey."

He really liked her. The success she was having with the Iowa Women's basketball team seemed to fit right in with all of the winning on campus. The 1985–86 season had been a good one for the women's team. They had won 9–10 down the stretch in the Big Ten (15–3). They had finished the season with a record of 22–7 and made it to the second round of the NCAA tournament, losing to Pat Summitt's Tennessee Lady Volunteers (73–68). It was a tough loss, but still a really good season. She sometimes brought her children to Carver Hawkeye, and Roy would play with them while the women were practicing.

The crowd had gone, and most of the people who remained were either on the custodial staff and finishing up the post game cleanup, or wrestlers. The dominance of Dan Gable's Iowa wrestling had been so great that it was almost expected that they would win every year. In fact, they had won nine in a row and eleven of the last twelve NCAA championships. Wrestling had been around since 1911. It was in 1976, when Iowa State wrestling legend Dan Gable took over the team, that things changed. Dan Gable was a winner on the mat before he stepped off to teach the next generation. He won NCAA National Championships in 1968 and 1969. In the 1972 Olympic games in Munich, Dan Gable won gold without giving up a single point in any of the matches. Earlier that year, in March, Iowa had won the NCAA Championship with 158 points, compared to second place Oklahoma's 84.75. Brad Penrith (126), Kevin Dresser (142), Jim Heffernan (150), Marty Kistler (167), and Duane Goldman (190) were all champions and continued the dominance that Hawk fans had grown to expect.

There was an air of winning in Iowa City, and everyone supported each other. The athletes became fans when their friends took center stage. Then they all met at the Sports Column and celebrated as a family. Roy thought about the year before as he headed to the bar. As a freshman he would go downtown, because that's where everyone hung out. The owner of the Sports Column, Mr. Mark Egelston, often stood at the door. He would talk about the game with Roy, and they got along great. The problem was, for a freshman whom everyone knew, one couldn't pretend he was legal to enter. Everyone knew Roy was eighteen, and Mark was no exception. He also knew that until December 13 rolled around, Roy couldn't get inside. Roy tried to talk his way in, but failed. Though disappointed, he respected Mark for sticking by the rules. When the faithful day arrived, at 12:01 a.m., Donny Stockfleet, a friend, gave Roy a photo to sign. They were standing outside the Field House at the time, but that photo was later framed and hung proudly on the Sports Column wall.

Ten

Brigham Young: Iowa Record (6–0)

Jeff Moe loved basketball. He had as long as he could remember, and this had fueled a passion for playing, whether playing in a game at Carver Hawkeye Arena or practicing alone in a gym growing up. This is how most high achievers reach their goals, especially in sports—they practice. They work hard with the team, they spend time on their own, and they go to bed thinking about getting better.

Crossover dribble, stop, his hand is in your face, elevate, and shoot. Repeat. Fast break, pass, or lay the ball off the glass. The decision must be automatic. Move without the ball, get open, make a target, catch the ball, and shoot. You're guarded, drive past the defender, then shoot or pass again. You're fouled, go to the line, stand there, alone in the gym, but more so than the last hour. Now it is quiet, just the ball bouncing in a steady rhythm. The foul is always a one-and-one because there is more pressure, and the game is on the line. Then it becomes a game of how many in a row—5, 7, 20? Keep going, keep shooting those free throws; they must become automatic. This was a life in the day of Jeff Moe, or Roy Marble, or the kid down the street who dreamt of wearing black and gold. Those days, they didn't care about your background, your race, your religion, or your gender. They just wanted you to try harder. It was the quest for improvement that defined the day and would define a life.

And yet, sometimes you went 2–8 from the field, as Jeff did in their last game. It didn't even seem possible that it could happen, but it did—in part because of good defense, and also because sometimes the ball just wouldn't go through the damn hoop. Those days were painful, less so if you won, but they always dug at you until you got to lace them up again.

That night a very talented Brigham Young team visited Iowa City. The Cougars (1–2) had played Oklahoma and Utah State, where they had scored more than 100 points in one win and one loss. Their last game was a defensive struggle, and they were held to 42 by Notre Dame in the loss. The previous season they had missed the NCAA tournament, but they had made it there in '84.

In the stands, a young boy, sitting with his father, read the program. "Jeff Moe, six foot three inches tall; he is a shooting guard. Do you know where he was born?"

The father, eating a handful of popcorn, said, "Was he born at the North Pole?"

"No! That is where elves are born. He wouldn't be six foot three inches tall if he were an elf, would he?"

The father, laughing, said, "No, he wouldn't. Where was he born?"

"Indianapolis, Indiana, on May 5, 1966. Which one is he?"

The father scanned the floor of players warming up and points. "See the guy shooting three-pointers? Yes, right there. That's him."

"I think he is going to be my favorite player."

"Why is that?"

"Three-pointers are awesome, and Uncle Roger lives in Indianapolis."

"That is a great reason. Want some popcorn?"

The game started, and both teams battled from one end of the court to the other. Iowa would take the lead, and Brigham Young would take it back. The crowd of 15,416, would erupt when Iowa pulled ahead and then just as quickly be cast into silence. The Cougars' Chatman, Smith, Capener, and Usevitch were giving as good as they had. The first half saw 12 lead changes and 4 ties with the largest margin being a scant 6 points. When they headed to the locker room for the break, Iowa was leading 45-40.

The Cougars started off strong in the second half, and after a little more than 2 minutes of play had closed to within two points, 52–50. Jeff Moe took matters into his own hands by sinking 2 three-pointers and a layup to push the lead to 60–50. Fifteen minutes remained.

Iowa, with outstanding shooting by Jeff Moe, pushed the lead to 15 points, but Brigham Young didn't give up. A nervous crowd watched as Iowa aided a comeback with some ill-advised passes and poor shots, and suddenly, with 2:00 left, the margin was only 5 points. Tom Davis called a timeout, worried that his players were letting it slip away. Brigham Young, needing to close the gap and conserve clock, chose to foul Jeff Moe and send him to the line. He made all four free throws to secure the win for Iowa and finish with a team high of 28 points.

After the game, Jeff said, "I went 2–8 in my last game, and I've been practicing too hard to let that happen twice in a row." He finished shooting 8–13 from the field and 9–9 from the charity stripe, and he pulled down 6 rebounds. Roy Marble and B.J. Armstrong added 16 and 15 points, respectively, to the effort.

The Cougar coach said, "Iowa is playing as well as any team in the nation right now. They certainly sold me that they are the No. 2 team in the nation. Not many teams go on the road to play Oklahoma, Notre Dame, and Iowa this early in the season. We're a better team for it."

The strong effort, albeit a losing effort, was good for Iowa, too. Facing adversity, especially late in the game, and showing the mettle to close out the win would be remembered the next time they were in a close battle. For the moment, the game was done, the season had begun 7–0, and they were ready to go meet Drake, on Saturday, in Des Moines.

Eleven

Drake: Iowa Record (7–0)

Most basketball arenas are built; Veterans Memorial Auditorium was born. On February 1, 1955, it opened and was named in honor of World War II veterans who were from Polk County. It has not been just a place to play basketball and host concerts; it has been a destination and a rite of passage for anyone who grew up in Iowa.

It starts with a bar of soap on a car window: Go Lions, or Cardinals, or Bulldogs, and then a group of teenagers pile into a car, travel the familiar gravel roads that lead to pavement, and from there they meander their way towards I-80 or I-35, and end in the state capital, Des Moines. They go to cheer their wrestlers, basketball players, gymnasts, and other athletes that crown their champion beneath the rafters of "Vets." As anyone who has grown up in Iowa knows, it isn't just the road trip or the outcome that matters, it is the joy of representing your school, town, and community. Regardless of the outcome, several school days missed means everyone is a winner.

Veterans Memorial Auditorium is a throwback to the middle of the twentieth century. It is big, and the cheering has a cavernous sound that is unlike any place around. The memories we all share of cheering for our favorite teams, be they high school teams, college teams, or the Iowa Barnstormers, always include the decidedly unique atmosphere that surrounds the game. It is big, yet comfortable, like an old worn blanket, and when we sit down to watch a game, we feel as if returning to visit a long lost friend. The ghosts of athletes and fans past are always present. We talk about the time we saw Kurt Warner resurrect his career, throwing touchdown after touchdown—so many, in fact, that it caught the eye of NFL scouts. It is a place one must visit to understand. It is a place that will always welcome you back with open court or mat or field.

Saturday Night and the fans fill up the seats, not all are sporting Drake blue and white, as plenty of black and gold can be seen. The Drake Bulldogs, part of the Missouri Valley Conference, has had a consistent history of playing great basketball. In 1971, coming off earning their third straight MVC title, won a close game against Houston, 92–87, to earn a ticket to the elite eight of the NCAA tournament. Though they lost to Kansas, 73–71, a heartbreaker in overtime, it was a season still talked about to this day. It was their third "Elite Eight" appearance. In addition, they had been to the "Sweet Sixteen" five times.

The night began with a Bulldog run, 15–2, that had the Hawkeye loyal sitting silently, listening to the enthusiastic home crowd and wondering when the Hawks would get on track. Miller had 2 three-pointers and Martin had one, for Drake, in the first 8 minutes. After that initial run, the Hawkeyes settled down, and through excellent rebounding, from Ed Horton (10) and Brad Lohous (8), were able to get back into the game.

When the final buzzer sounded, the Iowa Hawkeyes were just too much for the Bulldogs. The final score, 69–62, didn't really tell the tale of how close a game it had been. Drake actually outscored Iowa from the field, 56–53, but it wasn't enough as Iowa was a brilliant 16-of-20 from the free throw line, and this was the difference. The Bulldogs left Veterans with a 3–4 record, while the Iowa Hawkeyes continued to impress and pushed the record to 8–0.

Coach Davis said, "We have not been a very good free throw shooting ball club. If we had shot mediocre from the line tonight, we would not have won the ballgame."

Drake Coach Gary Garner said, "Rebounding was probably the biggest difference in the ball game. We didn't handle their press very well. Those were the two biggest problem areas for us."

The ride home is always better after a win, but after starting 8–0, the Hawkeye players and staff were feeling pretty darn good.

Twelve

Iowa State: Iowa Record (8–0)

The Iowa vs. Iowa State rivalry dates back to February 5, 1909, when the Hawkeyes won by three in Ames, 30–27. Iowa would win the first ten meetings until a loss on February 16, 1917, 24–12. Eleven days later, Iowa would take the interstate honors back by winning in Iowa City, 15–13.

The rivalry, before the tip, stands at 27–10, but ISU had won the last three, including a heartbreaking 76–72 loss in double overtime at Hilton Coliseum in 1984. Last year the Hawks fell 61–74, but this was not 1985. Iowa was the third ranked team in the nation.

It was easy to get excited for rivalry games, but for Roy, this was a special game. Playing for ISU was his childhood basketball friend from Flint, Jeff Grayer. By the time his career was finished, Jeff Grayer had set thirteen school records that stood for years, including scoring, with 2,502 points. He would go on to the NBA as the thirteenth pick overall in the 1988 draft and accumulate 3,257 points and 1,294 rebounds over his professional career. Even if Roy had been able to see into the future and foresee what lay ahead for Jeff, it wouldn't have mattered; he already knew that his friend had game.

Hilton Coliseum opened with a win against Arizona 71–54 on December 2, 1971. Named for James H. Hilton, it hosted basketball, wrestling, gymnastics, concerts, and—in the 70s—men's hockey. It also battled against floodwaters from the Skunk River and stood strong. A massive concrete structure, the building had great acoustics for the home fan.

The phrase hadn't been coined yet, but a few years down the road, Des Moines Register sportswriter Buck Turnbull wrote, "Hilton Magic Spells 'upset' One More Time" after ISU earned a victory against the number three-ranked Missouri Tigers on February 14, 1989, 82–75. The phrase stuck and inspired fans to cheer a little bit louder to bring home a win.

Patrolling courtside with Dr. Tom Davis was Iowa State head coach Johnny Orr. Coach Orr, no stranger to Big Ten basketball, had coached at the University of Michigan as an assistant until he was promoted to the top spot in 1969. In 1974, he guided the Wolverines to the "Elite Eight" and then, two years later, finished second in the NCAA tournament, losing to undefeated Big Ten rival Indiana. That year he was named National Coach of the Year. At Michigan he had a 209–113 record and then went to Ames to take the job of head coach in 1980. In 1985, he coached the Cyclones to their first NCAA tournament appearance in forty years. He would retire from coaching in 1994, amassing 218 wins and only 113 losses, and he would forever remain well loved in Ames.

On this night, however, it would be Coach Davis who would add one to the win column. The Hawkeyes jumped out to an early lead 12–2 before the Cyclones rallied back, but just as they were getting close, the Hawkeyes turned it up a notch. The score at the break was 52–34, and Iowa had only made three turnovers. With an 18-point margin, the Hawkeyes came out playing tough. There wasn't a point in the second half where ISU was able to get closer than the 18 points and, at the end of the game, the scoreboard at Hilton Coliseum read ISU 64–Iowa 89. The Hawkeyes were now 9–0 and proving that they deserved to be counted among the nation's elite teams.

Roy Marble had a solid game, with 11 points, but it was Ed Horton who really shined. In just 21 minutes, he was 8–13 from the field, making his only free throw attempt and wiping the glass for 11 rebounds. Horton led all Iowa scores with 17, while for the Cyclones Tom Schafer hit for 19, and Roy's buddy, Jeff Grayer, added 17. Iowa showed great depth up in Ames, with six players in double figures.

After the game, Orr said, "I have nothing but praise for Iowa," in the post-game interview. "They did a great job. I think they outdid us in every department. They wanted to win much more than we did. They deserved the victory—by the margin and everything else." When asked about the Cyclones, he said, "I was disappointed with my team's performance. We've been sputtering all year. We've not played up to our capabilities. I just hope we do it, or it'll be a long year."

Dr. Davis said, "I think that thing surprised us all. I think it surprised our players and our coaching staff. It was a combination of things where we just happened to play very well. We got great performances from a lot of people. And terrific intensity."

When Ed Horton was asked about his performance, he said, "I'll say it was one of my best efforts. I do say everybody was up for the game. Coach Davis did a great job of letting everybody know how tough a week it would be."

The week was a long one, indeed, because there wasn't only the work that needed to be done on the court, but also the work that needed to be done in the classroom. This was finals week at Iowa, which meant there wasn't a single practice that everyone on the team could attend. Finals were a part of being a student athlete, and when they were done, the Hawkeyes had made it through with flying colors.

Thirteen

Rider: Iowa Record (9–0)

Three days before Christmas the Hawkeyes faced their tenth opponent of the year, Rider, which was coming off its worst loss of the season, at Providence 106–66. The Broncos, from Lawrenceville, New Jersey, weren't afraid to schedule tough opponents and, though they had some close games, their record stood at 0–6. Facing one of the top teams in the country wasn't going to be easy.

Rider has one famous alumnus, Digger Phelps, who played for Rider from 1959–1963, and it would eventually have another, Jason Thompson, who would be the twelfth pick of the Sacramento Kings in 2008. Their colors were cranberry and white. They played out of the Metro Atlantic Athletic Conference and traveled to Iowa City to face a team coming off a great win against their interstate rival, ISU.

After the ISU game, Roy Marble said, "Going home for Christmas saying I'm undefeated—hopefully we will be after Rider—that feels good. That'll be my Christmas present." Iowa fans across the state and country, would agree that a 10–0 start makes the holidays joyful.

Any coach will tell you that you can't assume anything, so preparation for Rider was no less stringent than that for any of their previous foes. When they hit the court, it showed. Roy had a team high of 19. Coach Davis distributed the minutes to fourteen players with thirteen of them scoring at least one bucket. The final, 104–71, and Iowa had delivered the Christmas present Roy had hoped for.

Rider's coach, John Carpenter said, "It will take a heck of a team to beat them. They keep coming at you. It's the type of team you expect Tom to turn out." John and Tom had faced each other previously when they both coached in the East Coast Conference. He continued, "He used a lot of players, but I don't believe they played as well tonight as they did in the two games I saw on film and TV. You might expect that after an emotional win over Iowa State."

When Roy was asked about the game, he said, "We feel very confident right now, and it will be great to go home, because 10–0 is better than 9–1 or 8–2." And then he added, "I don't know how good a team we can be, but we want to keep improving until we are as good as we are in practice. We have some fine leadership. Take Brad Lohaus. He's doing a great job of leading us."

Al Lorenzen, who had been recovering from a leg injury, saw 15 minutes and scored 12 points. "I thought Al did a nice job. He's showing signs that he's going to be a player. I'm pleased," said Davis when asked about the junior from Cedar Rapids. The coach continued to speak highly of his team's performance: "I also like the rebounds and assists we're getting. Things like that help the team concept. We've got a friendly battle going between Lohaus and Horton for the team lead. I believe Lohaus was one ahead of Ed before tonight. First one who gets 100, wins the first part of the competition." Lohaus outpaced Horton 8–7 in that department, on that evening.

Fourteen

Portland: Iowa Record (10–0)

Christmas was over, and Dr. Davis took his team to Long Beach, California, where they were to meet the Portland Pilots. Portland had started off the season 3–4, losing their last two. A member of the West Coast Conference, they were coming off a 13–15 season.

Naturally, Iowa was favored in the opening round of the Anteater Classic, and perhaps expected an easy game. Portland was having none of it. They roared to a 15–4 lead behind the confident play of their pair of guards, Greg Attaway and Greg Anthony, both 6'3". Despite Iowa's bigger presence on the floor, the Pilots' speed forced Coach Davis to give up on the zone defense. Attaway scored a fearless 21 points in the first half, and the rest of the team shot an amazing 63 percent from the field. In a much tougher game than the Hawkeyes expected, they went into the break up a scant 4 points, 48–44.

The grumblings from the Iowa faithful gathered at the Sports Column back home were likely audible all the way to California. "How can a 3–4 team be hanging with our 10–0 Hawks?"

Dr. Davis had a word or two with his players and sent them back out for the second half. The boys from Iowa City started the second half with an 8–2 run to give them some breathing room. Kevin Gamble had 10 points in the first half and 16 for the game, to lead all Iowa scorers. The final, much to the relief of the Sports Column crowd, was 84–65. Iowa improved to 11–0 and got a bit of a wake-up call.

That is the beauty of basketball. If the shots are falling, a 3–4 team can run with one of the best teams in the country, even if for only a half. That is why they play the games.

Fifteen

California-Irvine: Iowa Record (11–0)

The Black and Gold were ready for a tough final in the Anteater Classic, but maybe not quite sure of what lay ahead. The cover of the media guide says a great deal about the attitude of U.C. Irvine basketball. It shows the team playing on a blacktop court next to a beach with the ocean and a whole lot of that California sunshine. People sit courted, in shorts, on folding chairs, watching. It is as laid back as one might expect, except for one thing, the guy taking it to the hole.

To say the Anteaters play an up-tempo style of basketball is akin to saying Jack Nicholas liked to golf. No, Jack Nicholas redefined golf, and the Anteaters run the fast break better than anyone around. It is a blistering pace that few teams can manage to endure or unravel.

It is fortunate that of all the teams who could have been invited, the Hawkeyes are one of the teams who know a thing or two about running with gazelles or, in this case, Anteaters.

Looking at the lines, the telling statistic is the number of minutes played by the number of players. Coach Davis went nine deep: Brad Lohaus (26), Roy Marble (23), Ed Horton (21), B.J. Armstrong (28), Kevin Gamble (29), Jeff Moe (18), Bill Jones

(13), Al Lorenzen (14) and Kent Hill (18), while Cal-Irvine also ran nine men out onto the floor: Joe Buchanan (34), Scott Brooks (37), Wayne Englestad (30), Mike Doktorczyk (27), Kevin Floyd (20), Mike Hess (14), Rob Doktorczyk (18), Frank Woods (13), Mark Warren (7). Eighteen players battled. Every single one scored, and sixteen of the eighteen pulled down at least one rebound.

Four thousand three hundred eighty people saw the race that day. They witnessed brilliant passing, amazing hustle, and a three-point shooting barrage (Iowa 5–12, 41.7 percent and U.C. Irvine 11–22, 50 percent). When the game ended, the number three team in the country was two points better, 105–103.

Roy, the tournament MVP, who had 28 points (6-of-8 from the line), 10 rebounds, and 4 assists, said, "I can't say if we would have lost this game last year. … We won some close ones last year. This year there seems to be an air of confidence. I think it has to do with a little bit more maturity."

The play between Roy and Ed really shined. In his 21 minutes of play, Ed fed Roy for 7 baskets. "Ed Horton seems to know me now," Roy said. "When you come together as a family, you start to think alike. The same thing with B.J. We're together so much. They know what I can do, and I know what they can do."

B.J. Armstrong, who had a touch of stomach flu in the Portland game, was 10-of-18 for 20 points. "Right now it feels pretty good. We believe in ourselves," he said after the game.

Coach Davis, perhaps sensing a need to bring everyone back to earth, said afterwards, "I think there's an awful long way to go for this ball club. It's exciting to be 12–0. I try to enjoy the ranking because the players love it. I'm trying to go along with it."

"I don't think we're ready for the Big Ten, but most coaches probably feel that way about their team. It's just a terrific league. Ohio State is picked sixth, seventh, or eighth. It'll be a struggle."

Later, he joked, "But hey, we've got twelve wins. And we don't have to give them back."

Sixteen

In 1939, the Big Ten's Ohio State University faced Oregon in the NCAA tournament finals, but came up short, 46–33. The next year, Indiana beat Kansas 60–42, and then in 1941, Wisconsin won the tournament. More recently, the Indiana Hoosiers beat fellow Big Ten team Michigan in the 1976 finals by twenty, 86–66. Then again, Indiana took home the title in 1981 with a win over North Carolina, 63–50. It is called March Madness, and the start of the Big Ten season has the men looking toward the mythical twenty win mark, for it is believed that twenty wins guarantees one a ticket to "The Big Dance." This isn't always the case, but having twelve wins before the start of the brutal Big Ten season is a great start.

The conference began with Chicago, Illinois, Michigan, Minnesota, Northwestern, Purdue, and Wisconsin in 1896 and, three years later, added Indiana and Iowa. The Ohio State University joined in 1912, while Chicago left in 1946. In 1950, Michigan State joined the fun. Iowa would begin its Big Ten schedule with a visit from the Northwestern Wildcats.

The year was 1851, and on January 28, the Illinois Legislature voted and approved Northwestern's Act of Incorporation, but it wasn't until 1855 that the school officially opened. Located in Evanston, its mascot is called Willie the Wildcat, and its official color is purple.

The Black and Gold have never started a season 13–0, and all that stands between them and this mark is the Northwestern Wildcats. Coming into the game, the Wildcats were 3–4, having just endured a brutal loss to twentieth-ranked Duke, 106–55. On paper, it looked like an easy win for Iowa, but the tough games out in Long Beach had taught them not to take anyone lightly.

Could the men from Evanston come in to Carver and pull off an amazing upset? No.

The Hawkeyes played hard, though the starters spent much of the game watching their teammates run the show. Both coach Davis and Roy Marble were suffering from bad colds, so the effort and play of the rest of the team was much appreciated. At the half, the score was 37–15, and the effects of Northwestern's star, seven-foot center Brian Pitts, missing from the lineup because of a broken hand, was evident. This was especially clear in the rebound margin, Iowa grabbing 49 to Northwestern's 19 boards. Gerry Wright was starting to get back into the flow of the game, after returning from his own broken hand. He pulled down 8 rebounds, 2 blocks, and had 5 points, including one of his trademarked "Sir Jamalot" moments with a dunk late in the second half.

Michael Reeves had a solid line off the bench for the Hawkeyes. He scored 10 points on 2-for-3 shooting and 4-for-4 from the line, all in only 12 minutes of play.

******

The final horn blew. The teams headed to their respective locker rooms. Coach Davis talked to the team. He never stopped coaching. The good and the bad were covered, though not in great detail, and then it was time for him to head off to speak to the press. Guys showered and changed, and during a winning streak, the post-game locker room was a happy place.

Phil Haddy or George Wine, who ran the marketing and sports information departments, escorted Roy and any other players who had had outstanding nights to the press room. There were questions, often not much different from week to week, and the answers felt a little bit canned, but it was part of the life. Roy wanted to give the reporters something they could use, and he was sincere in his answers, but he was also aware that—especially in the early Big Ten games—they would meet these teams one more time. It was important to be respectful to the opponent and humble in victory because one never knew when they would be sitting there on the losing end.

Division I basketball, especially in the Big Ten, was a game of getting position, holding position, and getting battered in the process. From the stands, watching the ball move around the floor, one scarcely noticed the banging going on away from the action. When a seven-footer gives you a forearm shiver to the kidneys or suggests another spot under the boards might be better with a powerful elbow, it leaves a mark.

Almost everyone who made it to the Big Ten grew up in gyms. They dealt with the pain of competition for a long time, and then, with the schedule and college life, they needed to stay on top of it to survive the season. Roy looked forward to the treatment. John Streif had taught him how to take care of his body. He had explained that in order to reduce the inflammation and bruising, one needed to spend time in the full body tub filled with water and ice. Roy thought it was a crazy idea at first, but he trusted John and gave it a try. It worked.

After most home games, it was Roy and B.J. soaking for a couple of hours. The other guys were long gone. When Roy and B.J. finally left Carver, they were alone. It was part of the life.

Seventeen

Wisconsin: Iowa Record (13–0)

Sitting at the number two spot in the Associated Press poll, the Hawkeyes hosted the Wisconsin Badgers on Monday, January 5, 1987. Wisconsin's starting five—Donny Jones, Rod Ripley, J.J. Weber, Mike Heineman, and Shelton Smith—all played 28 minutes or more. Off the bench, Sean Fleming and Kurt Portman, contributed 15 and 16 minutes respectively.

Iowa went much deeper into the bench with ten players seeing quality minutes and six others making it late in the game. This was the story of the game, the depth, because Wisconsin found its starters, J.J. Weber and Mike Heineman, had 4 fouls each with 13 minutes remaining to play. All told, Wisconsin was called for 26 fouls, including a technical by Heineman, while Iowa had 19 called against them.

It was a scrappy game, and Iowa went into the half with a slim lead of 43–39, The Badgers' excellent shooting from the field, 64 percent in the first half, gave Iowa all they could handle.

At the start of the second half, Wisconsin twice pulled to within two points before Iowa went on an 11–2 run. The Badgers continued to battle back, but Iowa would answer each time with runs of its own, and, at the end of the game, Iowa had a 78–63 win, its 14th of the season. Wisconsin fell to 0–2 in the Big Ten and 10–5 overall.

Coach Davis commented after the game, "I think you see why in my pre-game comments that I had so much respect for Wisconsin. They're very well coached and they have a tough, physical front court and experienced guards. That kid Heineman is very, very good. They have several dimensions. We saw that in our scoring reports. I don't know if I did a good enough job making you aware of that. But that is a fine Wisconsin team capable of beating anybody in the Big Ten."

Ed Horton had another nice game, with 16 points shooting 4-of-6 from the field and 8-of-9 from the free throw line. Brad Lohaus was the second leading scorer with 15 points. The three-point shooting wasn't their strong suit, and the final tally was 1 for 9 from behind the arc, but they did a nice job on the boards, with Lohaus and Gamble both pulling down 8 boards apiece. Gamble said, "I'm trying to get more leadership out of myself. We've got great scorers and great rebounders. I'm trying to do the little things to help us win."

Across Iowa City, from the ped mall to Pagliai's Pizza, people felt the excitement of perfection. They talked about the games over their morning coffee in towns like Lisbon, Mechanicsville and even at the breakfast tables of rural Yarmouth. From the Mississippi to the Missouri river, all across the "Hawkeye State," people rehashed each game, picked their favorite players, and worked out how their team was going to win the next one, and the one after that.

It was exciting to win the Great Alaska Shootout and capturing the Hawkeye Amana Classic felt great, too, but that win in Long Beach and the continued success made cold January in Iowa seem like the best summer day anyone could remember. Success makes the days brighter. It also paints a target on your beloved team's back. The UNLV Running Rebels were sitting atop the AP poll. They had been there for five weeks as Iowa earned its spot near the top of the mountain. It is where everyone wants to be. For those who may not have had championship dreams, their shot at knocking off the top-ranked Big Ten team provided inspiration that would make the rest of the way a battle for the Hawkeyes.

Coaches talk of facing adversity, and they preach against the letdown, but the realities are that nobody is up for every game. There will always be letdowns, and the question is, how will the team react when the shots don't fall, when the other team can't miss, and when legs are weary from carrying the weight of the Hawkeye nation day after day.

It isn't just the players who dream of getting the big win; the coaches feed off the games, too. They watch film, and then they watch it again. The hours are long, but it is something that only a coach can understand, or maybe an addict. They pour their hearts and souls into their players—teaching, motivating, and planning—so that their guys are just a little bit better prepared than the opponent's. The coach is responsible for calling the defense, seeing when it isn't working, changing it up, and going back again. Then, in the blink of an eye, they are on offense, the ball goes in, and it starts over. Should we play full-court press or slow up the tempo, run or walk, shoot or take it inside, focus on fouling out their big man or protecting our own?

Optimizing player performance is another responsibility. Each man is unique and motivated in different ways. Without understanding the team, one is unable to get the most out of them, night in and night out. And then there are the refs, who need to be prodded, attacked, kidded with, and sometimes pushed past the brink that leads to a technical foul. When it is all said and done, sitting behind the microphone at the post-game press conference, the preparation for the next game begins, with the right words, the praise of the opponent, and the avoidance of bulletin board material. It is a delicate balance, to be sure, and some will tell you there is never time to enjoy a win because the next game is always waiting.

This isn't the end of the responsibilities, however, as there are the people who market the team, fill the seats, feed the patrons, and create an atmosphere that helps break the will of the opponent. The band is there, playing the fight song as well as cheering and jeering, along with the rest of the crowd. If the crowd wasn't important, nobody would have ever written about, "Home Court Advantage," and there wouldn't be any need for cheerleaders.

That night Iowa won a hard-fought game against a talented team. It had the fans and no travel. The streak continued, but a team only plays half its games in the comfort of its own arena. Across the Midwest are nine venues where the Black and Gold will be scarce, where the cheers will come from Iowa mistakes, and the hard play of Roy and his teammates will be met with boos. It wasn't going to get any easier.

In the preseason rankings, those in the know picked Dean Smith's North Carolina Tarheels as the nation's number one team. It is hard to argue with the likes of Kenny Smith and Jeff Lebo in the backcourt, but would they miss the number one pick in the last NBA draft, Brad Dougherty? Dean Smith said that his team's rankings were overrated, but an impressive win over Big Ten Purdue, 94–81, showed they had the talent to be among the nation's elite.

Eighteen

Dr. Tom Davis's Hawkeyes would be facing another coach new to his program, Clem Haskins, hired by the Golden Gophers in 1986. Before entering the coaching ranks, Clem and Dwight Smith were the first black athletes to play for the Western Kentucky Hilltoppers in 1963. Haskins had taken over a program that finished with an 11–15 record, the Gophers losing their last eight games of the season. In 1982, they made it all the way to the Sweet Sixteen. Now it was up to Clem Haskins to bring the program back.

When one is rated number two in the country, it also brings out the opposing fans. Saturday, January 10, was no exception, as 16,104 fans showed up to cheer. Minnesota had also played Northwestern and Wisconsin, winning both games, though by a much closer margin. They were riding their own streak at 6 consecutive wins and stood at 7 and 3 on the season.

Clem Haskins, aiming to pull off a huge upset for his program, chose to house his players in a hotel for the three previous nights to allow them to focus on the visiting Hawkeyes. But in the end, the depth of the team from Iowa City was too much.

Point guard B.J. Armstrong picked up his third foul early in the first half, and, as such, Bill Jones and Michael Reeves came in and kept the Hawkeye team running smoothly.

Bill Jones played 20 minutes and made 2-of-3 from the field and 2-of-2 from the charity stripe to finish with 6 points. Coach Davis said, "We saw Billy Jones step in and do a terrific job. Our offense didn't miss a beat." Bill Jones, a guard, 6'7", from Detroit, Michigan, came off the bench repeatedly during the '85–'86 season. Shooting .482 from the field, and .802 from the free throw line, he scored 307 points as a sophomore.

When asked about the game, Jones said, "I was a little winded in the second half. In the previous two years up here, we came up kind of short. This feels kind of good."

Brad Lohaus, added, "Oh, man! Any road win in the Big Ten is good. I can't put enough importance on it. The team is extremely happy."

The defensive efforts of the Hawkeyes shut down Minnesota's sophomore, Kelvin Smith, who had been averaging 18 points per game and 8 rebounds. He left the floor with only 2 points and 0 rebounds. The final score of 78–57 gave Iowa a 15–0 record and made for a nice trip back home from Minneapolis.

******

Broadcasters talk about the depth of the bench. Coach Davis knew the value of playing time and had confidence in his bench. The bench was vital for a successful program. They were the guys who pushed the starters in practice.

Young players don't often think in terms of the big picture. Everyone wants to be a starter, so it is easy to try to focus only on individual stats, impressing the coach, and outdoing the guy ahead of you on the depth chart. Coaches, however, have been around a long time. They see the big picture and know who cares about the team. It isn't just performance that coaches remember, it is attitude, aptitude, and effort. Coaches never forget, either.

Bart Casey was as much a local as one could be. He came into this world with his fraternal twin brother, Bret, at Mercy Hospital in Iowa City, Iowa. Growing up an Iowa boy, he went to Regina High School in Iowa City. They were the Casey's second set of twins. Brad and Vicki, who were six years older, were the first. Bart was lucky, as he had an older brother who loved the game, too. Brad played with Mark Gannon on three state championship teams for Regina. He taught Bret the game.

Growing up, Bart was a shy kid. The Field House was his escape. It was where he truly fell in love with the game. He would spend all day playing, whether with others or just shooting alone. It was a safe area where he received positive feedback, which was what a kid who lacked self-confidence needed.

When George Raveling came to recruit Bart, the coach was rambling on about pride and such, when Bart said, "I was a Hawk long before you got here, and I will be a Hawk long after you are gone." Raveling was, as the saying goes, "preaching to the choir." Bart wanted to be an Iowa Hawkeye more than anything, and he didn't wait to be asked. He actively went after Iowa.

When Carver Hawkeye Arena was being built, Bart's father was a sub-contractor on the job. Bart worked on his father's crew and helped build the Arena. When the day came, nineteen guys showed up to camp, and there were only fifteen spots. Bart sold himself to coach Raveling, and it worked.

It may seem odd, a kid growing up in Iowa City taking a trip to visit the campus, but Bart did. He remembers how very strange it was the first time he rode there. Though the city and the university were intertwined, they were separate. It was a different world on campus. It was where Bart wanted to be, and when he got there, he invited his new family to meet his parents, siblings, and dog. The Caseys had a pool table and a German shepherd named Magnum. Magnum tipped the scales at around 100 pounds and was very excited to meet Bart's new friends. He wanted to play. To some of the other guys, though, the line between play and attack was a little fuzzy, and Magnum chased a few of them around the pool table before they were properly introduced.

The whistle blew. Casey, who had stretched out, was ready. Something clicked, and he briefly remembered his first practices as a Hawkeye. The speed, strength, and intensity of the college player were so much more than he had imagined. But now, he was here, helping the team, playing the game he loved. It is good to be a Hawkeye.

The practice started. It would run two-and-a-half, maybe three hours, sometimes longer. Bruce Pearl screamed in everyone's ear. Morgan and Marble got tangled up, and it started again. Horton and Jepsen started pounding on each other, and the play continued. It stopped, Coach Davis taught, explained, and then it started again. Armstrong and Reaves battled, banging on each other with a ferocity that, to a casual observer, looked like deep hatred. In fact, the intensity with which they played in practice was so great that Coach Davis started to cut the game situation time short during the streak for fear of injury. He had them spend extra time working on shooting, one-on-one coaching, and conditioning instead. If the guys came to practice with a pop in their steps and made their shots during the workouts, Coach Davis knew they were ready for the game.

Nineteen

Illinois: Iowa Record (15–0)

The streak would be tested on the road in Champaign, Illinois, against the fighting Illini, who were themselves, among the top programs in the nation at number eight. The eyes of the basketball nation would be watching when they tipped off Wednesday night.

On the southern border of the state, in Davis County, a town of fewer than three thousand people, Brady DeVore, eleven years old, sat in his parent's bedroom. He would be watching on their 13-inch black-and-white TV, which required an occasional smack to get the picture to come through.

In Iowa City, at the Sports Column, Angie Kremer, a student in her second year at Iowa, sat with her friends and some pitchers in a packed bar waiting for the tip.

Illinois won its first seven games of the season before a loss at North Carolina, 90–77. They also lost a heartbreaker at Loyola, 83–82 before winning their first four Big Ten games against Michigan, Michigan State, and on the road at Wisconsin and Northwestern. Now they were about to face the undefeated Hawkeyes. Their fans were whipped into a frenzy, all 16,666 of them.

The Hawkeyes, despite playing hard, were getting run out of the gym. Tony Wysinger and Doug Altenberger were making it rain for Illinois. Altenberger had 4 three-pointers in the first half. Everything they put up was right on the mark and, it seemed, there was little Iowa could do to stop them. Wysinger missed only once, making 19 of the Illini's 52 first half points.

Iowa's Brad Lohaus had 19 points, compared with the rest of the team's 16. Nothing seemed to be working on the defensive end, and when the horn blew to signal a merciful end to the first half, they trailed 52–35. It wasn't that they weren't playing hard; it was just that the Illini were on fire. In one play, Kenny Norton received an outlet pass and had only Ed Horton between him and the basket. He could have gone left or right, but chose to go over and threw down a monstrous dunk. The explosion of fan glee nearly brought down the house.

At a house in West Branch, Jon Miller, 15, watched the game with his family. They moved to town in 1979, just before Lute Olson took Iowa to the Final Four in 1980. He told his father, "I am going to be the 'Voice of the Hawkeyes' one day. Later in life, he studied Radio and TV and then founded the site www.hawkeyenation.com. But that day he was just a fan.

Most games, during halftime, regardless of the weather, Jon would go outside and shoot baskets in the back yard, pretending to be Roy or B.J. However, with his beloved Hawkeyes trailing by 17, he was inconsolable. He sat on the basement stairs while his parents, brother, and sister remained in front of the TV, waiting for the second half and hoping it would be better.

It didn't get any better when they returned to the floor. Jens Kujawa scored twice from the three-point range to push the score to 61–39, and now Iowa was looking at a 22-point mountain and only 16 minutes to climb it.

The mark of a championship team is not how they handle winning, but how they deal with adversity. All the Iowa fans across the state, especially Angie, Brady, and Jon, were still cheering and maybe praying a little, when the Hawkeyes started their run. B.J hit a jumper to get back to down 20 and then with 15:35 left, Jens Kujuwa, a 7 footer from Taylorville High School, missed a dunk. He looked rattled, as did his teammates as well as the fans, He would miss his next five shots. Iowa answered with 8 more consecutive points and had shaved the lead to 12. The Sports Column was rocking.

The clock still had 13:08 left on it, but would there be time? Lou Henson brought in a freshman named Kendall Gill and then, with 10 minutes remaining, Illini Wysinger, from Peoria Central High School, scored to push the lead back to 14, 69–55.

The coaching battle continued with Dr. Tom Davis continually guiding his players and encouraging them to fight on. Jeff Moe responded with a brilliant three-point shot just in front of the Iowa bench to cut the lead to 10. The Illini went cold. Gerry Wright, blocking a Tony Wysinger shot, was then immediately fouled. He went to the line and made them both, cutting the lead to 78–71. Only 4:23 remained.

With 3:35 remaining, Gamble hit a short shot from the baseline to cut the margin to 3. Roy Marble, with lightning reflexes, stepped in and stole the inbounds pass, drove to the bucket, and dunked it. The score stood 78–77.

Jon Miller was ecstatic, as were Angie and the screaming fans at the Sports Column. Brady was praying the TV would hold out.

Only 42 seconds remained, and the score was tied at 81 when Gamble fouled Glynn Blackwell from Highland Park, Michigan, a spectacular free throw shooter. He had made his last 24 in a row. He missed the front end, and neither team could put it away in regulation. Overtime!

Marble made one of two to get the first points for Iowa in the extra period, and Horton grabbed the rebound on the missed shot. Horton was fouled by Doug Attenberger, and went to the line where he went 1–2. Tony Wysinger nailed a three-pointer for Lou Henson's team, and the score stood at 84–83, Illinois, with 3:48 remaining in overtime.

Iowa missed its next shot, and the Illini were out running on a fast break. Only B.J. was back, and he drew the charge from Wysinger. B.J. hit both free throws to give Iowa the lead.

Blackwell scored with 2:15 left to play, making it Illinois 86, Iowa 85. Horton turned the ball over, and Moe committed a foul on Blackwell. The 90 percent free throw shooter returned to the line for a one-and-one. Again, he missed. Iowa pulled down the rebound and called time-out. The clock read 1:29.

A short while later Gamble blocked Wysinger's shot, and it led to a layup by Roy. Iowa leads, 87–86. Ken Norman answered for Illinois, and with only 32 seconds remaining, the No. 8 team was back up by 1, 88-87. The clock ticked away, and B.J. Armstrong nailed a long two-pointer to give the lead back to Iowa.

Wysinger tried to feed the ball to Norman with time running low, but Kevin Gamble deflected it to Brad Lohaus who was immediately fouled. Lou Henson chose to burn a time-out, one of his two remaining, to ice Lohaus. Lohaus would NOT be iced, and made them both. Norman had a final shot from three-point land to send it into a second overtime, but it didn't fall.

Dr. Tom Davis described the locker room scene: "I was literally speechless in the locker room afterwards. I've never seen anything quite like that. To struggle like we struggled and to see our guys come back like they did, it was just hard to believe."

Iowa remained unbeaten, and fans everywhere still remember the bar, or steps, or old black-and-white TV that was a part of that game, part of their youth, part of Iowa lore.

******

Roy was the second of four children, his older sister's name was Theresa, and then there was La Shema and Jeron. His mother, a religious woman, would often pray for her son and his team to play well. When Iowa was losing in the second half of the Illinois game in Champagne, his mother told everyone else watching that she couldn't take it anymore. She went to her room and prayed herself to sleep. When she woke up, Roy's father told her that they had won, and she said, "God has answered my prayers."

Twenty

It had been five days since the Illinois game. Now they had to travel to Mackey Arena in West Lafayette, Indiana, and face Gene Keady. Hired in 1980, from Western Kentucky, he had guided the Boilermakers to a 22–10 season in 1985–86, finishing fourth in the Big Ten.

To say he picked up where he left off the previous season would be a great understatement, as Purdue climbed all the way to number two in the nation before getting beat 94–81 at North Carolina. They haven't lost since, and their record stands at 14–1, 5–0 in the Big Ten.

Iowa, coming off one of the most impressive comebacks in school history, had five days to prepare for their meeting. Purdue, on the other hand, had hosted the Louisville Cardinals the previous night, winning 88–73. That said, Gene Keady would have his players ready. The fans would be ready, too, all 14,123 of them.

In a matchup that pitted the Nation's number one-ranked team, Iowa, against Purdue at number five, all eyes were on West Lafayette. The Hawkeyes had been unsuccessful in their last five trips to Mackey Arena, and this test would possibly be the toughest of them all. Last year, when the Hawkeyes made the trip, Purdue won the game, 76–73, and then, later that year, Iowa took them at home, 77–64.

Purdue came out strong, led by Troy Lewis and Todd Mitchell, who poured in 12 and 11 points, respectively. The tough Purdue defense forced eighteen turnovers by the break. Despite Iowa's rebounding edge, 20–13, and fine play from Gamble, 9 points, and Moe, 8, the Hawkeyes trialed 38–42. This was life in the Big Ten. The play was aggressive, the pace was fast, and with 11½ minutes remaining in the first half, Roy was hit in the eye by a pass from Jeff. The Hawkeyes' three-time tournament MVP would spend the rest of the game on the bench with a patch over his eye.

It was always a battle when facing Purdue. Roy, when lacing them up before the game, got his mind right. Purdue games were always physical. They play hard, have a lot of talent, and seemed to always be up for playing the Hawkeyes tough.

While sitting in the locker room with a patch over his eye, a lot of things crossed Roy's mind. The one thought that kept bubbling to the surface was, "I can't believe that Moe passed the ball." Jeff was a 'gun slinger,' and everyone knew when he came in the game he was coming in firing. Nine out of ten times, he took the shot. Roy replayed it in his mind. The pass was heading for Jeff; he instinctively started to battle for position, to get the rebound, should Jeff miss. Roy remembered the open spot, looking up at the basket wondering where the ball was, and then Moe made a quick pass. Roy saw it and tried to react, but the ball was already only a foot-and-a-half from his face. He got his hand in front with just enough time for the ball to drive his thumb into his eye. The pain was sharp and burning.

He couldn't see out of his eye. The trainers, worried he might have scratched his cornea, decided on the patch, with plans to wait until they got back to Iowa City to have an expert look at it.

Shooting a basketball into a hoop is a complicated affair. The brain sees the distance, judges the depth, and then tells the muscles exactly how much force to apply for the shot. Shooters all have different mental methods of going through the process, but the key is being able to see. With just one eye, it would be the end of Roy Marble's career.

Roy tried not to think about the worst-case scenario and, though he certainly could have felt sorry for himself, mostly he just didn't like sitting out of a basketball game. First and foremost, he wanted to play, but Roy trusted the coaches when they said he was done for the day. So he wore a patch and cheered for his teammates.

The second half started, and Iowa did a better job of taking care of the ball, but still had 12 turnovers. They pounded it inside and worked the glass, taking only 4 three-pointers during the entire game and making one. Purdue was much more active from long range, putting up 17 shots, but only Doug Lee and Troy Lewis connected, making two each. The game was a battle, and neither team seemed to be able to find the bucket near the end. Kevin Gamble scored from just outside the lane with a little over 4 minutes remaining to give Iowa the lead, 67–65. Neither team scored for the next 3½ minutes.

With 27 seconds remaining, Ed Horton threw down a dunk and was fouled by Everette Stephens. Ed went to the line and made it to give Iowa a 70–65 lead. Melvin McCants took advantage of a missed shot and put the ball in to close the game to within one possession, 70–67. Twelve seconds remained. B.J. Armstrong was fouled immediately and went to the line for a 1-and-1, but missed the front end. The fans were going crazy. Troy Lewis had two shots from three-point land, which would have sent it into overtime, but missed. Iowa remained perfect.

Kevin Gamble had played a great game, shooting 90 percent from the field, (9-of-10) and pulling down 8 rebounds.

Roy left that night happy but worried. An eye injury can be devastating to a shooter, and he tried not to think about worst-case scenarios.

Twenty One

Indiana: Iowa Record (17–0)

During the 1965–66 college basketball, Army finished the season 18–8, and Bobby Knight's career was underway. In 1971 he moved to Bloomington, Indiana, to become the Hoosier head coach, and an institution was born. In the fall of 1975, the Indiana Hoosiers started the season atop the AP poll, and coach Knight guided his team to 32 wins and an undefeated NCAA title, running the table. 1981–82 he added another National Championship.

It seemed that he was always right there, coaching, teaching, and leading his men toward victory. That's why they called him "The General." January 22, 1987, the cream and crimson will visit the top-ranked Hawkeyes. Indiana, sitting in the number three spot on the AP poll, will head into Carver Hawkeye Arena hoping to take what Iowa has—the top spot.

The University of Iowa Men's basketball program has never played a home game while ranked number one in the nation. Coach Davis, before the game, said he thought that Indiana was the best team in the country. Was he being honest or trying to soften them up?

The key to Indiana's offense was a kid from New Castle, Indiana—6'2" Steve Alford, who was shooting 70 percent from beyond the three-point line. Iowa was going to need help from everyone, including their own Indiana boy, from Indianapolis, sixth man Jeff Moe. The biggest concern among the Black and Gold faithful was the status of Roy Marble and his eye. He hadn't practiced as much as normal but was out warming up, so the crowd was cautiously optimistic.

The players are announced, the referees—Bob Showalter, Ed Hightower, and Sid Rodeheffer—were ready, the ball was tossed into the air … and both players missed it. Take two, Horton controls the tip, but Indiana ends up with the first possession. The crowd starts immediately to chant, "Let's Go Hawks."

Indiana is moving the ball around the perimeter; Iowa is playing a tight man-to-man defense, and then Keith Smart drives the lane, only to miss. Ed Horton recovers the rebound. The first trip down the floor for Iowa ends in a missed shot from Kevin Gamble. The ball, almost out, is tipped out of bounds, and the original call is overturned. Iowa ball. Thirty seconds into the game, and The General is already in the faces of the officials.

Marble goes inside, is fouled by Daryl Thomas and heads to the line, making them both. Indiana misses, B.J. runs the break and makes a nice bounce pass through the Indiana defenders to Horton, who dunks it with authority. 4-0, Iowa. Steve Alford takes his first shot of the game, just inside the three-point line, misses, and before Indiana knows what hit them, Armstrong to Kevin Gamble for a layup.

Both teams battle back and forth, and the crowd stays involved. Brad Lohaus fouls inside, goes to the line, and makes the first but misses the second. Horton is there for the rebound and takes a nice eight-foot jumper, making the score 9–1, Iowa.

Dean Garrett takes the pass, makes a nice move, and hits a turnaround jumper for Indiana. 9–3, Iowa. Iowa starts to run, a three-pointer, long, and Indiana rushes back to the other end, four-on-one break, missing. Roy pulls down the rebound, kicks it out, Armstrong to Moe, and he is fouled inside. Jeff, an 80 percent free throw shooter for the year, makes the first one. The second bounces around some and decides to fall, to put the score at 11–3 after 5 minutes of play.

The atmosphere inside Carver Hawkeye Arena is electric. A black balloon is being bandied about, the Iowa fight song fills in the gaps between play, and everyone is enjoying the 8-point lead.

Keith Smart takes the pass on the wing and elevates to drain a jumper. Indiana pulls to within six, and the bucket gives them time to get back on defense.

Jeff Moe takes a three-pointer from just above the top of the key, misses, but Al Lorenzen is in perfect position to pull down the offensive board. The ball is stolen but sent out of bounds, so Iowa gets it back on the baseline. Bobby Knight, 18–10 versus Iowa, paces the sideline in his scarlet Indiana sweater.

Bill Jones comes into the game. The Hawkeyes spread it out, passing around the perimeter. Indiana tries to trap Jones, but he gets the ball to Moe, who puts up a shot that hit off the front of the iron. Moe follows his shot, pulls down the rebound, takes one dribble, and lofts a beautiful shot in over the leaping defenders. Iowa leads, 13–5. Indiana pushes the ball up, Iowa steals it in the lane, and as soon as that happens, Bill Jones starts sprinting the other way. He receives a perfect pass and throws down a crowd-pleasing dunk. Iowa, 15–5.

Iowa switches to a full-court press, but Indiana recognizes it and makes an inbounds pass to half court. Alford brings it up quickly for a two-on-one break, kicks it out to Dean Garret, the 6'10" junior from San Clemente, and he hits a nice baseline shot that rattles in. Iowa 15–7.

Iowa passes the ball around the perimeter and then Jeff Moe drives, and it hits off the back of the iron. Indiana goes for the rebound, but Moe is in there battling; he ends up on the floor, and Indiana passes out of the scrum. Keith Smart, the 6'1" guard from Baton Rouge, Louisiana, races down the floor, and Bill Jones is forced to foul. The foul is on the floor, so Indiana takes it out of bounds. They pass it in and move it around until Joe Hillman, a 6'2" guard from Redman, California, has it near the top of the key. He passes it cross-court to Calloway in the corner, who takes a quick dribble and tries to float it in and misses. The rebound is contested by several players, and eventually Indiana comes up with it, and the Hoosiers reset their offense. They work it around until Alford puts up a three-pointer from well beyond the arch and makes it to cut the lead to 5. Alford is shooting 58 percent from the three-point range (70 percent in the Big Ten), on the season. As a team, Indiana leads the nation from beyond the arc, at .575 shooting percentage.

Iowa brings it up quickly, shoots, misses, and fouls on the rebound. The Iowa defenders lose track of Calloway, and he makes an uncontested jumper from the baseline. Iowa leads, 15–12.

Indiana battles for the rebound off an errant shot from the baseline by Iowa. The ball gets kicked out of bounds, and it goes to Indiana. Alford takes the inbounds pass and drives, but the Hawkeye defense is in position, so he pulls up and dribbles it back outside. He passes over to Hillman, who sends it right back to Alford. Three more passes, and the ball is back in Alford's hands. He puts up a three, misses, and Marble comes down with the rebound, immediately turning on the jets.

Marble draws the defenders, makes a pass to Horton, and is credited with the basket on a Dean Garrett goal tending call. Iowa, 17–12. The full-court pressure works. Armstrong steals the ball but is immediately called for traveling. The crowd disagrees with the men in black and white. 12:00 remains, and the players gather at their respective benches for the television time-out.

The long arms of Brad Lohaus make getting the ball in difficult, but Indiana eventually breaks through and gets it over to mid-court. Alford passes to Todd Meyer, who gives it back and sets a pick. Alford comes off the pick and passes. Indiana is really moving the ball around well. Iowa's defense is matching them step for step, and the shot clock winds down to 20 seconds.

Finally, Calloway puts one up from the baseline, but Marble is in his face, and the shot is short.

Jeff Moe with the ball at the top of the key sees his "seven footer" under the basket and puts up what looks like a shot but is actually a perfectly aimed pass. Lohaus easily makes the bucket to push the lead back to seven.

Indiana struggles to break the pressure, but after they get it past the mid-court stripe, B.J. is called for a foul, his first and the fifth on the Hawks.

Keith Smart returns to the floor for Indiana and immediately puts up a shot with Lohaus in his face. It is good, Iowa, 19–14.

B.J. brings the ball up and moves to the right side of the floor. Jeff Moe rotates to the top of the key, where he receives the pass. He immediately sends a bounce pass inside to Horton, who has it stripped away by Joe Hillman. Hillman starts up court and loses control of the ball. Moe corrals it, passes it to B.J. who sends a perfect pass to Marble … dunk … cheers. Iowa, 21–14.

Indiana quickly breaks the press, and Daryl Thomas, the 6'7" forward, makes a nice move to the bucket for two. Iowa, 21–16.

Armstrong takes a pass on the right side, quickly goes up for a shot and misses, but Roy is there for the put back; he has six on the day. The crowd is thrilled.

Indiana quickly strikes, and Daryl Thomas gets another basket. Iowa, 23–18.

Armstrong gets a bounce pass along the baseline and shoots. It takes a long bounce, and Jeff Moe is there. He takes the jumper, misses, Horton is there for the rebound in among a crowd of Crimson and Cream, and is fouled by Joe Hillman while in the act of shooting. He goes to the line. Ed Horton, on the season, is 32-of-55, or 58 percent from the free throw line. He swishes the first. He makes the second and raises his percentage to 59.6. Iowa 25–18.

Indiana's Alford gets trapped in the corner, but manages to pass out of trouble. Dean Garrett quickly gets to the baseline, turns, and makes it.

Iowa set up, makes a few passes, and then Jeff Moe drains a three-pointer to pull Iowa ahead by eight, 28–20.

Alford, on the run, stops and pops from beyond the three-point line; the ball bounces around until Al Lorenzen grabs it. At the other end, Horton is fouled by Keith Smart, but not in the act of shooting, so Iowa takes it out on the baseline. After a time-out, Gamble takes the inbounds bounce pass under the basket and lays it in. Iowa leads by 10.

Indiana moves the ball around. Jeff Moe chases Alford all over the court and, despite Alford's best effort, is unable to shake him. Indiana gets the ball inside; Lorenzen goes up but fouls. The crowd thinks it is clean, but they don't get a vote. Indiana takes it under the basket, tosses it out to Calloway, who is near the top of the key, and Bill Jones skies for it. Foul on Calloway, his third. Iowa ball.

The game is moving at a steadfast pace. They run, bang, move, cut, pass, shoot, rebound, and the clock runs. Watching the game, fans of both teams wait for the moment, the turning point, when their beloved cagers will take control, but this isn't a game between also-rans. This is a game between two of the finest programs in the country, coached by two basketball scholars.

Smart hustles to cover Bill Jones, but he is too aggressive and runs into him for the foul. Bill goes to the line for the one-and-one and makes the front end. He is shooting 71 percent for the year from the line. The second one is short, but that is fine. Kevin Gamble has his back and puts in the rebound. It is Iowa's eighth offensive rebound of the game, while only giving up two to Indiana.

The Hoosiers bring the ball up, and Smart is fouled by Gerry Wright. Before play resumes, Ed Horton, Roy Marble, B.J. Armstrong, and Brad Lohaus all come back into the game after a breather. It is hard to tell the starters from the bench as Iowa is playing such a seamless game regardless of who is on the court. The Iowa bench has outscored the Indiana bench, 10–0. Smart makes them both. It is now Iowa 33–22.

B.J. gets it into Gamble, who goes up against Garrett who has been a presence for Indiana, inside. He has, year-to-date, 40 blocked shots. The point is moot, however, as Keith Smart fouls Gamble. It is his third. Smart heads to the bench, and Knight sends in Tony Freeman, a 5'7" guard from Westchester, Illinois, in his freshman season. Gamble, shooting 70 percent for the year, misses the first of two but drains the second one. Iowa expands its lead to 12 with just over 6½ minutes remaining in the half.

Indiana slows the pace by passing around the perimeter. The fans are chanting, "Let's Go Hawks." Sloan goes baseline and passes it to Garrett for an easy two, his eighth point of the game. Gamble takes a quick three-pointer that misses, and Garret pulls down the rebound. Alford comes off a screen but fails to connect. Horton gets the rebound, and they head the other way. A long pass to Marble, but before he can do anything with it, he is fouled into the third row of fans by Brian Sloan. Marble, at the line, sends the ball to the rim where it debates whether it should fall, finally deciding to pass through the net. The second shot goes straight through. Mable has 8 points in the first half.

A flurry of activity at center court and finally Thomas scores for Indiana but comes down hard off of Wright's back. He gets up slowly and jogs to the other end of the floor. Iowa brings the ball up and then the whistle blows. Steve Alfred and Jeff Moe are battling, and Moe is called for the foul away from the ball. Alford, 90 percent career free throw shooter, steps to the line and sinks the first one. The '83 Mr. Basketball in Indiana makes the second one, and the lead is cut to eight.

Iowa's Mr. Basketball from Indiana, freshman Mark Jewel, watches from the bench as Iowa brings it up the floor. Indiana in a man-to-man defense gets the ball back on an Iowa foul, Roy's second. Garrett goes to the line and puts up a shot that could best be described as a brick, but Sloan is there for the put back. Iowa 36–30. The constant cheering from the Iowa fans remains unwavering.

Lorenzen misses, Horton rebounds but misses also. Garrett gets the ball, posting up, but Horton is in position, and the shot is off the mark. Horton grabs the rebound. A traveling call on Moe gives the ball back to the Hoosiers.

3:58 remaining in the first half.

Iowa continues to apply full-court pressure. Indiana gets the ball in, and Alford brings it up the floor. A few passes, and Garrett gets the ball inside, again, and makes the bucket. Iowa 36–32.

Lohaus takes a shot, but it is off the mark. A half dozen hands fight for the ball, Marble gets it, dishes to Lohaus who takes a ten-footer and drains it for his fifth point of the game. Brad rushes to cover the inbounds pass with his long arms. The pass is quick and then another pass, but B.J. Armstrong steps in and steals it. A moment later, Freeman fouls Kevin Gamble, who heads to the line for two and makes them both.

At the other end, Freeman gets loose at the free throw line and sinks an uncontested shot. Iowa turns the ball over at the other end, and Indiana is back trying to close the gap. Kevin Gamble is called for holding, and Alford goes to the line for a couple of automatic points.

B.J. is called for charging, and the cheers turns to groans.

Thomas trips, but Lohaus is called for a foul. Daryl Thomas continues the Indiana comeback and cuts the lead to two points, 40–38.

Horton takes a long jumper, misses, and Brad Lohaus flies in and dunks it with authority. The crowd approves enthusiastically.

Garrett throws down his own dunk at the other end, and the game is back to a 2-point margin. 1:20 remaining in the half.

The ball is stolen, Freeman runs the break, and Thomas gets an easy layup. The game between the number one and number three teams in the nation is tied at 42.

Lohaus, with a 15-foot jump shot, passes the ball and then gets it back. The Indiana defense doesn't react, and he nails the easy jumper. Thirty-five seconds remain in the half, and it looks like the Hoosiers will hold for the last shot. The whistle blows as Ed Hightower sees something on the court. Coach Davis takes the opportunity to substitute Roy, Kent, and Bill back into the game. On the end bounds pass, Bill Jones nearly picks it off. Seventeen seconds remain. Before Indiana can inbounds, though, Jones is called for a foul away from the ball, his second. Brian Sloan, a Mr. Basketball from Illinois, hits them both.

Iowa runs a pick and dishes the ball off to Marble, who drains a three-pointer to give Iowa a 46–44 lead. The desperation shot by the Hoosiers is close, but doesn't fall. It was a hard-earned three-point lead for the nation's number one team.

The first half in the books, Iowa shoots 46 percent from the field, and Indiana puts up an impressive 59 percent, but Iowa out-rebounds the Hoosiers 25 to 9. In the end, though, the score is still 46–44, and it doesn't matter how they got there, but how they finished.

The second half begins, Iowa ball, and quickly they get it down low to Brad, who puts it in for a quick two points. Indiana brings it down quickly, passes to Alford on the wing, who hits a comfortable fifteen-foot jumper.

Bobby Knight sends one player in to make the inbounds play a little uncomfortable, but Iowa handles it and gets the ball in to guard B.J. Armstrong's hands. He brings it up and calls the play. A quick two passes, and then it is in to Horton who takes it up strong, through the Indiana defenders, and puts it in. Iowa 50–46.

Tony Freeman, running the point for Indiana, has kept them in the game. He moves the ball around. Indiana is doing a lot of running, picking, and eventually he gets it inside. Thomas scores and is fouled. He makes the one-and-one. Iowa 50–49.

The game has slowed in pace. Both teams are looking for good shots. Horton misses, but then at the other end, Calloway hits, and Indiana takes the lead for the first time in the game. But it doesn't last long. Brad Lohaus takes a jumper from just inside the top of the key to put Iowa back up 52–51.

Indiana answers with a drive down the baseline for an uncontested dunk by Calloway. Neither team seems to be able to stop the other. Indiana 53–52.

Tony Freeman picks up his second foul, preventing Marble from an easy two. The Hawkeyes lob the inbounds pass to Horton, who is blocked. The ball is heading out of bounds when Lohaus jumps and throws the ball back in, as if to bounce it off of the leg of Alford to save the possession. Kevin Gamble snatches the ball as it bounces up, turns, and takes it to the hole before anyone knows what has happened. Iowa 54–53.

Iowa continued with the full-court press, but Alford gets the pass and easily makes his way across center court. He throws it to Freeman, who drives the lane and misses, but Garrett is there for the put-back.

Lohaus, at the other end, a foot outside the three-point line, shoots, but it is a bit too strong. Three Hawkeyes go up for the rebound and end up knocking it out of bounds but off a Hoosier–Iowa ball. The inbounds pass catches Indiana sleeping, and Alford is forced to foul. It is his first. Ed Horton heads to the line and makes them both. He has 12 points. Kent Hill checks into the game for Horton after he makes the second one.

The pass into Alford is nearly a three-quarter-court pass. He has a two-on-one break, makes a nice bounce pass to Calloway, who puts it in—Indiana 57–56.

The Hawks move the ball around the outside, swinging it from one sideline to the other, then B.J. steps forward, elevates, and drains it with the foul. Tony Freeman picks up his third. Armstrong hits the bonus, giving him a three-point play and his first points of the contest.

Indiana gets the ball up court quickly, and Kevin Gamble picks up his second personal foul. Daryl Thomas, the second leading scorer for the Hoosiers, steps to the line and makes the first one. He averages 15 points per game. A 73 percent free throw shooter, he makes it, his fifth of five from the line, and scores 15 for the night. The score stands at 59 all.

Faced with a switch by Indiana to zone defense, Iowa moves the ball around, looking for an inside opening, but as the clock winds down, Jeff Moe fires up a three-pointer and hits it—Iowa 62–59.

Tony Freeman, sprinting down the court, makes a nice pass, and Horton is forced to foul to prevent the easy bucket. Thomas will returns to the line for a chance to bring Indiana back to within one. When he is done, Thomas is still perfect from the line, 7 for 7.

A long skip pass to Jones, who takes it over Garrett, but it bounces off the rim and out to Kent Hill. Up once, misses, but follows his own shot and gets the put-back. Indiana quickly gets out on the break, a three-on-two, but the Hawkeye defense is up to the task. The ball heads out of bounds, off of Iowa, so Indiana will get it back underneath. Indiana tries to pass it to the top of the key, but Iowa steals the ball, and Jones and Moe are sprinting to the other end. After a miss, Marble puts it in, putting Iowa up by five, 66–61.

The cheering of the crowd, constant since the half started, has found another level. People are on their feet. It looks like the Hawkeyes are feeding off the energy. Indiana tries to get out quickly, again, but it is blocked, and now they have numbers at the other end. Brad Lohaus pulls up at the three-point arc, shoots, and misses, but is called for an over-the-back foul on Freeman as he tries to pull down his own rebound. It is his third foul.

Alford takes the inbounds pass, moves the ball up, and eventually Freeman pulls up for a ten-foot jumper, but it comes up short. Iowa grabs it, and Jeff Moe tears down the court with Alford waiting. A nice little move, and Moe blows past Alford for an easy layup. Iowa 68–61.

Coach Davis still has his players using the full-court press, and Alford is having trouble finding a Hoosier to pass to. He runs the baseline, but Lohaus is there with him, step for step. Alford finds a narrow gap and makes a bounce pass through the defense. Calloway takes it to about nine feet, stops on a dime, pulls up for the jumper, but can't hit. Indiana's Garrett and Al

Lorenzen battle for the ball; the ref blows his whistle, signaling Indiana ball.

With 18:39 remaining in the game, a time-out is called. The Iowa bench has outscored Indiana's bench by eleven, 17–6. Coach Davis has gone deep into his bench all year, and it has given them confidence to play, even in the big games. Indiana has the ball under the basket, but the press is too tough, and they turn it over on a five-second call.

Iowa, faced with the Hoosier man-to-man defense, swings it around the outside, looking for a good shot and showing some restraint. After a half dozen passes, Horton takes the bounce pass, turns, and sinks it. Iowa is up by 9.

The Black and Gold continue to show high energy playing their full-court press. Indiana gets the ball in and pushes it up court. Iowa does a good job of preventing the pass down low and keeps Steve Alford from having a big night. Indiana continues to pass the ball around, and B.J steps in and gets the steal. He immediately passes it up ahead to Marble, who lays the ball up, but it bounces a few times on the rim and out. Kevin Gamble, with great hustle, has followed on the play and is there for the tip-in. It is effort that is winning the game for Iowa.

The Hawks immediately trap on the inbounds pass so as to keep the pressure on the Hoosiers. Calloway has to throw the ball off of Marble's leg to get out of the jam. This has the crowd even more fired up, and everyone is on their feet. Iowa leads, 72–61.

Lorenzen deflects the inbounds pass, but it goes right back out of bounds. Indiana retains possession. They are really having a hard time with the pressure. Will Iowa be able to keep up this pace?

Dale Thomas for Indiana takes the ball from the ref, and Iowa goes about trying to prevent the pass. He sends a long pass across mid-court to Keith Smart, who has a two-on-one break, and he takes it to the bucket. Indiana is back to within 9.

Iowa sets up, and Lorenzen takes it at the top of the key. Indiana is almost begging him to shoot, so he moves in a little closer. They still seem unimpressed, so he takes one more step, the IU defense jumps, and he makes a beautiful pass to Armstrong for an easy layup.

The crowd, still cheering the Armstrong bucket, erupts when Jeff Moe steps in, steals the inbounds pass, and lays it in for two more. Iowa 76–63.

Kevin Smart takes a three-pointer, misses, and Armstrong comes out with the ball, running. He takes it all the way to the glass for two, pushing the Iowa run to 19–4.

Finally, after the long drought, Steve Alford puts up a smooth three-pointer and makes it. The crowd takes a much needed breath. The Hawkeyes, however, do not. Armstrong brings the ball up; his team is quickly under the basket; he pulls up and makes the jumper.

Garrett tries to play inside, puts it up, but the shot doesn't have enough on it. Horton and Daryl Thomas tie the ball up. Jump ball, but the arrow indicates it is Indiana's ball. Still, great effort on Horton's part, and the next one goes to Iowa.

There is a time-out with just over 10½ minutes left to play, and Iowa has a nice lead of 80–66.

After the time-out, Iowa brings in four sets of fresh legs; Indiana keeps the same five on the floor. The depth of the Iowa bench makes all the difference—that and, of course, the thundering cheers from the crowd. Indiana comes off the time-out, and Garrett hits a turnaround jumper—Iowa 80–68.

Indiana had a good turn on defense and forces the turnover. If Iowans know anything, it's that "Counting chickens before they are hatched is not to be done." Ten minutes is a long time, especially with the likes of sharp shooter Steve Alford on the visiting squad.

Smart takes the inbounds pass and gets a two-on-two break. He shoots and misses. Iowa, ball going the other way. Moe misses the three-pointer, but his quick hands allow him to bounce the rebound off a Hoosier's leg. Iowa retains possession. On the inbounds pass, Indiana's Brian Sloan fouls. His second. Was fatigue starting to become a factor? Iowa looks like they had a lot more in the tank than Indiana.

Marble passes it into Moe, who sends it over to Jones, who dribbles out to set up the play. Before Iowa gets anything going, Daryl Thomas fouls away from the ball, Indiana's fifth team foul and his second of the game. Davis makes a quick substitution, B.J, in for Bill Jones.

B.J. takes the inbounds pass and, from the corner, drains a three, but Alford answers with his own three at the other end. Iowa still leads by twelve, 83–71.

A turnover and Indiana has the ball. Alford elevates and looks to be shooting another three, but it is a pass to Smart, who makes an eight-footer. Indiana starts to crawl back into the game.

Iowa does a nice job of running some clock until Marble is open inside, and he gets an easy two. Again, Iowa stays with the pressure and earns a five-second call. Indiana returns the favor and, through tough defense, gets Iowa to make a mistake, sending the ball out of bounds. Indiana has it back and would try, again, to get it in bounds. They fail. Another five-second call against the Hoosiers.

Iowa succeeds in getting the ball in. Keith Smart tries and fails to draw a charging call, instead getting nailed for blocking. He has 4 fouls on the night. When Iowa gets the ball in, it is quickly tied up, and a jump ball is called. Iowa possession so they are back to the sideline trying to get the ball in play. It has been so long since there has been any basketball played that some of the players have graduated and moved on to grad school, while several people in the crowd have married, had children, and sent them off to Iowa, all while waiting for someone to get the ball in bounds. At the current pace, they are projected to finish near the turn of the century.

What all of this has done is to give the Indiana guys a bit of a breather. Iowa gets the ball in, and Jeff Moe travels with it while going to the basket. Indiana ball, out of bounds. The crowd has long since sat back down, and some of the energy had disappeared. The Hawk fans want to get back to some excitement.

Steve Eyl comes into the game for Indiana. The General has been doing a great job of using all the whistles to substitute, thus slowing the pace considerably. No longer are the guys in Crimson and Cream with hands on knees sucking air. They seem to have recovered during all of the out-of-bounds folly. And it continues. The Hawkeyes refuse to make it easy and immediately trap Sloan in the corner. The ball is tipped out of bounds, but still not to mid-court. Finally, basketball resumes.

Alford brings it across the center line, and the crowd begins chanting "Defense!" Thomas finds some space inside the lane and makes a nice jumper. Indiana is within 10 points.

At the other end, Iowa is passing, controlling the ball, and working the clock, and Steve Eyl, away from the ball, fouls. Al Lorenzen goes to the line to shoot the one-and-one. He hasn't spent much time at the free throw line that year, only making 15 of his 28 attempts, but swishes the front end. He misses the second one, and Indiana gets the rebound.

Indiana almost throws it away, but the quick hands of Alford save it to his man underneath, who gives it right back, and Alford puts up the three. He makes it, cutting the Iowa lead to 8, 86–78. The cheering sounds a bit nervous.

Iowa is again careful with the ball. They know what they want and continue to pass and move, looking for the high percentage play. The shot clock is down to 15; Bill Jones takes the ball and calls the play. He hands the ball off to Moe, who doesn't hesitate to shoot a bomb from well beyond the arc, and makes it. A great trip down the floor, they use most of the shot clock and push the margin to eleven, 89–78.

Jeff Moe gets called for a foul, but Indiana isn't in the bonus yet, so they take it out. Indiana gets it into Alford. He passes the ball, but Iowa's quick hands tip it off a leg, and the ref emphatically pointed Iowa's way. Indiana doesn't give on defense and gets the ball back on an Iowa travel.

The Hoosiers break the full-court pressure by sending it into Freeman, who sends it over to Alford. He puts up a three and makes it. The lead is eight, again.

Iowa works the clock and gets it near the five-minute mark when Tom Davis calls a time-out.

B.J. throws the ball into Lohaus, who puts it up but is blocked. Brad picks up his fourth personal foul, trying to get the ball back. Indiana brings the ball across the mid-court line, and the Hawkeye defenders make an effort to prevent the ball from getting into Steve Alford's hands. He has made 5 three-pointers for the day, including four in a row, and is the biggest threat to getting Indiana back into the game. Alford dribbles beyond the arc, eyeing the basket, but the blanket-like defense of Armstrong makes him think better of shooting. Iowa continues to play tight defense and forces the ball out of bounds. It is Indiana's possession, but only 6 seconds remain on the shot clock. A lob pass to Garrett, and he quickly shoots a ten footer, good. Iowa clings to an 89–83 lead.

Iowa runs about 25 seconds off the clock, and B.J. gets a good look from the baseline. He makes the shot. Iowa is back up by eight.

Alford, nearly trapped in the corner, gets the ball to Freeman, and Indiana gets moving on offense. Freeman makes a quick pass into Daryl Thomas, and he takes it up, making the bucket and getting fouled by Lohaus, his fifth. Lohaus fouls out with 13 points and 3 rebounds. Al Lorenzen is sent into the game by Davis. Thomas makes the free throw. Iowa still leads 91–86 with 3 minutes left to play.

Iowa gets the ball inside to Lorenzen. He takes it up but misses. He is first to the rebound and fires it up again, scoring. The Hoosiers break the full-court press, and Lorenzen fouls Freeman at the other end. He makes them both. It is a five-point game with only 2:20 remaining. Indiana's Sloan quickly fouls Roy and sends him to the line. He misses the front end, but Horton grabs the rebound. Iowa runs the clock under the 2-minute mark, and then Lorenzen is called for a charge. The crowd is getting nervous.

Iowa tries to trap, but Indiana gets free and passes the ball around until it ends up in Alford's hands. He fires a three from several feet beyond the three-point line and hits nothing but the bottom of the net. Then the crowd erupts, and the ref runs in and calls Alford for stepping out of bounds. The basket is waved off—Iowa ball.

Armstrong dribbles the ball casually. Indiana is a little lax in setting up its defense, expecting Iowa to run the shot clock all the way down. Armstrong sees an opening and beats everyone to the basket for a layup for a 95–88 lead. Indiana brings it up court quickly. Alford fires up a long shot but misses. Horton is fouled by Garrett on the rebound. The players walk back to the other end.

Fifty-nine seconds remain, and coach Bobby Knight calls a time-out. After the time-out, Horton misses the front end of the one-and-one, and Indiana gets the rebound. Indiana quickly takes it to the hole, misses, and an outlet finds Marble all alone. He dunks it with authority. The crowd roars.

Indiana brings the ball up, but it is stolen. Iowa is still playing like it is a two-point game and rushes to the other end. Gamble adds two more points. After another stop, Gamble gets another basket and is fouled with 5 seconds remaining. Though he misses the free throw, it doesn't matter, and Iowa, the number one team in the nation, has just beat the number three Indiana Hoosiers, 101–88.

It wasn't just a win to defend Iowa's position atop the college basketball mountain, it was the eighteenth win in a row—the longest streak in program history.

After the game, when asked about the repeated comebacks by Indiana, Davis said, "That's why it was a terrific college basketball game, because they kept coming back. We couldn't put them away, but I didn't expect anything less from Indiana."

Asked about the waved off three-pointer, coach Knight said, "We were just a couple of inches, with Alford stepping out of bounds like that, from being right in the ball game." Knight assessed the game by saying, "We were down by something like 62–61, and they got that spurt and went up something like 68–61. You have to be really careful to avoid that, and we tried to but they just kept at us. That made it really tough to come back."

Davis had high praise for B.J Armstrong: "B.J. played an outstanding game against some very complicated defenses. He showed great alertness out there."

It was a great night for Iowa and a not-so-great night for Bobby Knight and his Hoosiers. The 101 points topped the previous most a Knight-coached team had surrendered. When Knight was a coach at Army, they lost to Boston College 92–85 in 1966, and then when he was at Indiana, they lost to Michigan 92–73 in 1978. The Hawkeyes had simply showed up to play and had finished off a tough stretch against three of the toughest teams in college basketball.

Next Up: Ohio State

Iowa City is a wonderful town, full of art, culture, restaurants, and bars. On the worst of days, one can still find a good meal, meet interesting people, and feel at home. These were NOT the worst of days. Wherever one went, the talk was of the streak.

A table of twenty year olds, drinking a pitcher and waiting for a pizza at the Airline, talk about the way Iowa has handled the top teams. A voice of reason talks of let downs, but is quickly mocked into submission. Comparisons are made and possibilities considered.

At the Deadwood, through a haze of smoke, people who generally prefer discussing late nineteenth century literature put down their books and begrudgingly admit to being fans. It feels good, and the pride a town or a state feels when they are taken along for the ride is hard not to love.

In dorm rooms at Burge Hall, Hillcrest, or Mayflower, freshman guys revel in Hawkeye glory in the hopes that their displays of enthusiasm will impress the women. The women don't notice because they are too busy cheering themselves. Maybe a few notice. All are in agreement, "Hawks Rule!"

In the classroom, students who might be fading, who may have lost interest in the historical significance of the work of Caravaggio, may be brought back to the present with a deftly placed basketball reference. "Though he was the most famous painter in Rome from 1600–1606, I doubt he ever came back from 22 down to Illinois, (pause for cheers), still, he was a good painter and it will be on the mid-term." This may have been the type of thing one would hear in late January, were one an art history student.

It didn't matter who you were or what you did, if you lived in Iowa City that winter, you were along for the ride. The days between games were great for the fans. For the guys, at least, when the brain wasn't focused on food or women, it would fill in the gaps with visions of steals, dunks, amazing runs, and broken-spirited opponents crushed under the running feet of the number one Hawkeyes. The dream would start with just another win, then it would add in the rest of the Big Ten games, and by the time lunch rolled around, the Hawkeyes had won the NCAA tournament three years in a row and shattered John Wooden's winning streak of 88 games. The only thing that could stop the daydream madness at that point was a girl in a tight sweater.

Still, the streak hadn't been all runaway successes. Iowa had played hard, trailed often, and overcome some very good teams to collect those victories. It was a fine line between best in the nation and middle of the pack in the Big Ten. The Iowa players knew it, but the fans knew only two numbers: one, as in their rank, and eighteen, as in their streak.

Twenty Two

Saturday, January 24, 1987, at Carver Hawkeye Arena. The fans gathered to watch their undefeated Iowa Hawkeyes play the unranked Ohio State Buckeyes. The Scarlet and Grey came to Iowa City with a record of 13–6, 3–3 in the Big Ten. They had won three in a row.

It had been an up and down season for OSU. They had lost to in-state opponent Dayton, by three, but had also gotten a nice win against Kansas from the Big Eight. They would be ready to play. This would be their chance at glory.

Roy was feeling tired, and his feet were swollen and sore. His body hurt, and the early game time made it all the worse. The fans would expect a walk in the park, especially after the last three wins, but Roy knew it was going to be a battle. All the games were.

The Buckeyes, despite having six more losses than the Hawkeyes, did have some very talented players, especially Dennis Hopson, a 6'5" senior. As a junior, he had averaged 20.9 points per game, shot nearly 80 percent from the line, and had 1.6 steals per game. Thus far in '86, he was doing better in all those categories. Roy and Dennis knew each other from previous meetings and they had developed a bit of an on-court rivalry. There was no love lost between the two.

The Hawkeyes played hard, but in the end, it was Ohio State—behind their senior Hopson, who had 36 points—that came away with the victory, 80–76. There would be no joy in Iowa City that night.

The headline in the Cedar Rapids Gazette read, "Home Is Where The Heart Breaks," and the article by Mike Hlas summed up the feelings of the Hawkeye nation when he wrote, "It was fun while it lasted."

After the loss, coach Davis said, "I certainly have no illusions that we are just going to walk out there and beat these other teams. We've got our hands full every time we step out there. And to the credit of our ball club, we had won them all coming in. But we knew we had our hands full the rest of the year every night out."

When asked if his players were flat, Davis responded, "You never know how much of that is because the opponent played really well. Our opponent played really well against us. I was worried our players didn't realize Ohio State ranks right up there with Illinois and Purdue and Indiana. I don't know that they recognize that. I tried to tell them about the team winning the NIT, and that they were better than other Big Ten teams at the end of last year, and that Hopson's the best, and that Gary's going to do as fine a job as you can do on the bench with them. … I don't know that I was heard but that's the plight of teaching.

Sometimes you've got to understand that. Some days you're not going to be heard."

When asked about the Buckeye's speed in breaking through the full-court press, Davis said, "They're very quick. There wasn't any one thing we should have done to stop them. They played superior to us in every way."

Brad Lohaus said he thought there was trouble brewing at half, despite the game being tied at 41: "After the first half, everybody knew it. They were hungrier than we were, they were out hustling us, diving for the loose balls."

Though everyone was disappointed, B.J. Armstrong, who led the Iowa scoring with 20, said, "This won't hurt us. It'll be a test for us to see how tough we really are. We'll just have to come back and be mentally tougher than we were today."

"I wouldn't call it a letdown game. We just couldn't get it going for some odd reason. This is definitely a setback for us going toward our goals, which is to win the Big Ten. We just have to evaluate ourselves."

This wasn't the end of the world, though. The pall that hung over the Iowa locker room was understandable, but the character of the team was not shattered. They had not been run out of the gym; it had been a close game. They made only 6 of 14 from the free throw line for only 42.8 percent. Basketball is a tough game, and on this night a great team faced a hungry opponent, and the Hawkeyes played ever so slightly below their norm. It happens in sports—there is variance, there is good luck, there is bad luck, and sometimes you lose.

This was the Big Ten. There wasn't time for licking wounds because in five days, Michigan State would be waiting in East Lansing.

Twenty Three

Forty-seven miles from Roy's hometown, Flint—just down
Highway 69 past Swartz Creek, Durand, and Perry—lies East
Lansing, Michigan. In East Lansing that month one found
Michigan State University and its basketball team, coach, and
fans awaiting the Hawkeyes in Jenison Fieldhouse.

Jenison Fieldhouse, built in 1940, was a throwback of an arena.
With its beautiful brick facade and pitched roof, it housed up to
10,004 fans, most of whom would be cheering for the Spartans.
A few from up the road, however, would be yelling for Roy and
his Hawkeye teammates.

The Spartans, who were having a tough year after having finished
third in the Big Ten the previous season, planned a special night
in the hopes of inspiring an upset victory against the number
two-ranked Hawkeyes. They would be honoring former Spartan
great Scott Skiles, who had set the record for most points scored
at MSU in a season at 850. Over his career he had poured in
2,145 points. He was the twenty-second pick in the 1986 draft by
the Milwaukee Bucks.

There was an air of excitement about the place, because everyone
knew that Iowa had shown it could be beat. A win against

number two would be just the sort of thing to turn the season around. Standing at 7–10 on the season, Michigan State had just lost a heart breaker at Northwestern 65–67 the night before. They had, however, beaten the Buckeyes 90–80, and since Ohio State had just beat Iowa, the math seemed to indicate that they had a chance.

But this wasn't math class.

Now, there was always the naysayer, the pessimist, the mud slinger in the bar. He may not even have been an Iowa fan. He may have been from Ames or someone who grew up rooting for the Buckeyes, but he took great delight in pointing out anything negative about the Hawkeyes. This guy had little to talk about that season, but he clung to the Hawkeyes' ranking second worst in the Big Ten in three-point shooting. He brought it up every chance he got.

That night he said nothing.

The game started out in typical Big Ten fashion, with the teams tied at 10 apiece. Kevin Gamble and Jeff Moe decided to put an end to the naysayer's go-to insult, and they each buried 3 points as part of the Hawkeyes 16–3 run midway through the first half. Iowa continued to shoot from outside, hitting 7-of-13 for 53 percent from three-point range. Michigan State tried to match the Hawkeyes, taking 14, but only making 4. Kevin Gable made 3-of-5, Jeff Moe was 3-of-4, and Brad Lohaus hit 1-of-3 to help Iowa get back on the winning track.

After that run, Michigan State was unable to shrink the margin beyond 7. Iowa got back to its winning ways with an 89–75 win.

The leading scorers for Iowa were Kevin Gamble (19) and Jeff Moe, who had 15 points in only 17 minutes of play. Another positive sign for the Hawks was the 21 minutes from Gerry Wright who had 8 points on the evening.

The Hawkeye skipper said afterwards, "I was worried about the game because I didn't know how our kids would respond after a loss. After winning so many in a row, we hadn't experienced defeat in a while. But I was happy in the way our kids bounced back."

The fans back in Iowa were as well, except for the contrarian in the bar.

******

Roy fell in love with basketball at a young age, as so many who excel at the game do. He loved Dr. J—Julius Erving—as a child, but it was one singular moment that made him decide it was a game he could devote his life to playing.

In 1976, Roy's first cousin Kinney McCarty played for Flint Beecher High, the same school Roy would soon attend. Flint Beecher had its own winning streak that year. At one point, against River Rouge, they were down by 20 at the half. His cousin and future high school battled back and won, preserving their winning streak. Roy never missed a game, and that one stood out as one of the most exciting he had ever seen. It was the moment he knew basketball would change his life, would become his life. Kinney's team went on to stay perfect, winning 27 games and losing 0, en route to a State Championship. The excitement and excellence Roy witnessed stayed with him, was the foundation for his work ethic, and truly did change the course of his life. Roy's 1985 high school team went 27–0 and won the State Championship, too. It was the school's second one in basketball.

Twenty Four

Davis, in talking about the upcoming game and the loss to Ohio State, said, "I think it will probably bother B.J. a little more than the other two. Roy has always risen to the occasion when the spotlight has been on him, and B.J.'s handled it pretty well and Bill, too. So, I hope they will use it to motivate them and that it will be positive."

After the game, he said, "I thought we kept making runs at them, and they would find a stopper. They would hit some free throws, make some good defensive or offensive plays and just wouldn't let us get back in the game there in the second half."

Gary Grant respected Iowa's run-making ability and said, "We knew an 11- or 12-point lead wouldn't be enough. We saw them come back against Illinois and Purdue."

Iowa had three nice runs during the game, but the Wolverines, led by Rice's 33 points, kept beating them back.

Bill Frieder, the Michigan coach, said, "There are just too many times the press doesn't come out and say both teams played well.

They played one hell of a basketball game, and we had to play a great game to combat them."

Michigan's Glen Rice had a fantastic game. He poured in 33 points and pulled down 10 rebounds, while teammate Garde Thompson had 24 points and 4 boards. Iowa saw a good game from Kevin Gamble who scored 22 and also led the team with 7 rebounds. The bench certainly helped by adding 20 points. The Hawkeyes actually had a better shooting percentage, 55.5 percent to 49.3 percent, but it just wasn't enough and the impressive 84 percent from the free throw line, was better than Iowa's 66.7 percent, which was a difference of 7 points.

In front of 13,609 fans, the Wolverines came out hot, leading 14–4 early in the game. Iowa answered with a 21–8 stretch that put them ahead 25–22 halfway through the first half. Michigan's Thompson responded by nailing 3 three-pointers, and they were right back on top by 7. A steal and three-pointer, right before half, gave Michigan a 10-point lead at the break.

The second half was more of the same and, despite their best efforts, they just couldn't find the magic they had found in Illinois. The final was 100–92 and gave Iowa its second loss.

It was Brad Lohaus who drew Glen Rice as an assignment for most of the game. "He played an outstanding game. I think he just got hot. I know he's averaging 16 points, but things were just falling."

Roy had about a hundred fans from home at the game and, when asked about any rivalry between him and the other Flint natives, he said of Rice's play, "That was the best I've seen him play in a while. It's always that competition, but I don't get into that. I'm proud of him, and I'm glad he's playing good. I live in Iowa City, and I'm not worried about what goes on in Michigan."

Twenty Five

Minnesota: Iowa Record (19–2)

19–2 is a good record. 1–2 over the last three games, well, that is upsetting. Nobody said it was going to be easy. It was time for the Hawkeyes to dust themselves off and get ready for the Golden Gophers of the University of Minnesota. It was a Wednesday, hump day as some might call it, and it was time for the Hawkeyes to get over the hump of their recent setbacks.

The cover of the Minnesota Golden Gopher media guide that year featured a pensive looking Clem Haskins with his suit jacket slung over his shoulder as he walked through an empty arena. One wonders if he was thinking about the 21-point loss that Iowa had issued on its home court earlier that season. It was time for him to face the same team—a team that was angry after the Michigan loss—in front of the Hawkeye faithful who also had some angst to vent.

It was not a close game. Iowa had two 10-point runs in the first half and held a comfortable 51–27 lead. The Gophers were well on their way to their eighth consecutive loss. The 14-point win in the first half was surpassed with a 17-point second half win to make the final tally 78–47.

It wasn't all bad news for the Gophers, as they had three players in double digits, Jim Shikenianski (13), Roy Gaffney (10), and

Willie Burton (10). In the Gopher's defense, they played hard and did hold Iowa to 78, which is no easy task, especially for a young team.

On Iowa's ledger there was plenty to talk about, but what really stood out was the play of Roy Marble, limited that it was. Roy only saw 25 minutes, but led all scorers with 14 and pulled down 9 rebounds. After the game, Roy said, "I'm trying to get more active. I'm really trying to make myself more visible." Asked another question about his assessment of his play, he responded, "I would say I've played on a consistent level, but not at the level I want. I want to increase my steal, rebounding, and defensive play. I'm really trying to bring that up. There's no special way. You just go out and try to pump yourself, and do what you can do."

Tom Davis was pleased with his team's play and especially liked Roy's comments. He added, "If I'm a pro scout, I'm saying, 'That's my kind of player.' We know he can score, and he's gonna be a nice outside shooter eventually. But those guys that can also pass and are willing to pass and also play 'D' and rebound, those are special people. And Roy has all those qualities." Davis then continued by saying, "This was the best Roy's played in a long time. I thought you saw vintage Roy Marble in the first half. Just terrific passing. He took the shot when he had it, and he made some unbelievable passes."

Twenty Six

Arizona: Iowa Record (20–2)

Winters in Iowa can be on the chilly side. It is quite possible that this was taken into consideration when someone added Arizona, on the road, to the schedule. Well, more likely, it was a case of reaching out to Lute Olsen, the former Iowa coach who was now down guiding the Wildcats program.

Any program's success, in some ways, is built upon the successes of old. There is value to having banners hanging from the ceiling, in being able to tell of the teams that came before and show new recruits the vision for what will come with their help. It is about painting a picture that makes it clear to the young man that this is the place for him.

It wasn't long before Roy arrived that Lute Olsen was patrolling the bench. In 1980, he had names like Ronnie Lester, Mark Gannon, Kevin Boyle, Vince Brookings, Kenny Arnold, Steve Waite, Steve Krafcison, and Bobby Hansen. Those names will be forever linked to Iowa basketball and what could be done with talent and effort.

In the 1980 NCAA tournament, the Iowa Hawkeyes earned a 5 seed and had to face 12-seeded Virginian Commonwealth. They had to travel to Greensboro, North Carolina, but it was worth the trip, as they made it to the second round with an 86–72 win.

Their prize was a tough battle with North Carolina State, who had the home court advantage. Still, despite the cheering fans, Iowa won 77–64. Next, they had to face the East Regional top seed Syracuse, coached by Jim Boeheim, and they were up to the task. Iowa won, 88–77. It was only John Thompson and the Georgetown Hoyas who stood in the way of Iowa's first trip to the Final Four since 1956. Iowa had a stunning 1-point victory, shooting 17-for-21 down the stretch and 15-for-5 from the free throw line. They earned a trip to the Final Four with the 81–80 win. Iowa would end up finishing in fourth place with a loss to Big Ten rival Purdue, 75–58. It was Denny Crum's Louisville Cardinals, with a 59–54 victory over UCLA, who crowned the National Champions that year.

Though one always likes to win the last game, in college basketball people remember how far one goes in the tournament. They remember Final Four appearances, and they don't just celebrate the victor; they tip their cap to all who made it to that last weekend.

A brief departure from the Big Ten schedule to battle a team from the Pac-10, especially one with ties to the school, is always nice. And there is the weather thing, too. In Eastern Iowa the average temperature in February likes to hover between -8 and 5 degrees. There is often snow, excessive wind, and the occasional Yeti feeding on travelers trapped in ditches by the wind and snow. Tucson, Arizona ranges from 41 at night to 68 in the daytime in February. People with advanced degrees in climatology will tell you that this range means it is a Yeti-free zone. But the Hawks weren't going there to soak up the sun.

They were going to face a tough Wildcat team who had just come off impressive wins against Arizona State (home and away) and Oregon.

Marble 7 points, 5 rebounds, Lohaus 14 and 9, Gamble 20 and 4, Horton 5 and 6, Armstrong 11 and 2, Wright 15 and 3, Moe 15 and 1.

They did it again. Iowa was down by 13 points in the second half. The 13,377 Wildcat fans were thrilled, but it didn't last. Iowa won; 89–80.

Davis credited the Arizona offense with their early deficit: "What got us down was they just played terrific. They were hitting all their shots and they were moving the ball well. We just couldn't find them out there. I even asked the coaches, 'What should we do?' I didn't know what to do."

Down 64–51 with only 11½ minutes to play, Iowa pulled out one of their patented runs. They ripped off a 25–4 streak, and when the dust settled, were leading 76–68. It all began when Armstrong nailed a three-pointer and immediately followed it up with a steal, which he passed to Kevin Gamble for a layup. Marble had 6 of his 7 points during that run.

Lute Olsen said afterwards, "There was no question when the game was decided. They got their transition game going, and I don't think we competed as hard as we had been in terms of getting back on defense."

Arizona didn't quit, though. They got to within 3 points after a nice Craig McMillan three-pointer, to make the score 76–73. He had 18 points for the Wildcats, second only to Elliott with 25. The game was still in doubt at the 1:23 mark when a pair of free throws by Ken Loften closed the gap to 83–80. Iowa, though, didn't crack and made all 6 free throws down the stretch.

Twenty Seven

All teams face it in conference play. The second go-around. The first time, especially in a close game, the losing team develops a bit of a grudge. The players dwell on it, mull over what went wrong, and consider how they might have done things just a little bit differently. It is in the DNA of every athlete and for the Purdue Boilermakers, the foul taste left in their mouths after the three-point loss in their own arena made them a dangerous foe. The score was close enough that they knew they could beat the Hawks, but it was also galling enough that it made them want to all the more.

The perspective from the winning team is always a bit different when you've already won, especially on the road; it is hard to wrap one's head around the possibility that the opponent has any chance in your house. Coaches don't think this way. They do their best to point out the perils of overconfidence and implore their players to focus, but alas, the argument is tough to make.

Iowa, now 20–2 and still in the hunt for the Big Ten title, would face a Purdue team in much the same boat with only two conference losses. A win for either team would help considerably toward earning that title. Purdue was ready and ranked seventh in the nation.

The first half was a close contest. Purdue jumped out to an early lead, 13–6, but Iowa battled back and closed it to 32–31 with 3 minutes remaining in the half. Sadly, the Hawkeyes couldn't wrestle the lead away from the Boilermakers and went into the break, down 39–35. Still, not an unmanageable margin, the crowd had confidence their team would come out firing in the second half.

It was the junior from Purdue, Everette Stephens, who came out firing. He made his third three-pointer of the game to start the half and Purdue was back to a 7 point lead. Though the crowd was noisy, their team didn't manage to get closer than 5 points the rest of the way, losing their third game of the year, 80–73, and putting their Big Ten Title hopes in serious jeopardy.

Everette Stephens had a great game for Purdue; he scored 23 points with 5 three-pointers and added 3 rebounds to lead all scorers. Mel McCantis had 16 points and 12 rebounds, while Troy Lewis put in 18 with 5 boards. For Iowa, the points were more evenly distributed with Lohaus and Moe having 14, Marble 11, and B.J 8. All eleven players who saw minutes for the Hawkeyes scored, including Michael Morgan who had one minute and two points. In the end, it was the long-range shots that let the Hawks down. They shot only 5–16, for 31.3 percent from beyond the arc. Had they been able to match their 50 percent plus shooting against Michigan State, they would have won by 2, but alas, Purdue was a better team, and the pressure made the shots more difficult.

In the post game, Davis said, "That Purdue team is first rate in every way. Their zone hurt us, but so did their man defense. They just outplayed us. Yes, it was physical. But it was just the kind of game you'd expect with two top teams playing an important game. Both teams really got after it."

"I think, perhaps, we do too much reaching and grabbing and not enough moving the feet and body on defense. We've been working on that."

Gene Keady, in an understandably good mood after the game, said, "This was the biggest game we've ever had on the road. I can say without hesitation that this is the best team we've played. We finally had all eight guys working together. This was a win we had to have to stay in the race."

He summed it up pretty well. When two great teams play, and one gets all the parts moving perfectly at the same time, the other will come away empty handed. Iowa didn't play badly. Purdue just played a little bit better.

Twenty Eight

Illinois: Iowa Record (21–3)

From the N100s of Hillcrest dormitory to the apartments on S. Johnson, enthusiastic students were coming home from class and getting ready for the game.

He walked home, carrying his backpack over one shoulder; the thoughts of his abysmal performance on the quiz having been pushed from his mind. "I wonder how Illinois is going to play?" he thought. "They are probably pretty pissed off. If we can just get out to a quick lead, maybe make some threes and shut them down with the press." He imagined the Hawks winning the tip, firing up a three, hitting nothing but the bottom of the net. Of course, Roy stole the inbounds pass and was fouled when throwing down a monster dunk. He made the free throw and it was Iowa up by 6 in the first 10 seconds of the game. That would have been great. He smiled at the girl who sold him the twelve-pack of Milwaukee's Best Light. She was cute, with black hair and painted black nails. He liked the Goth look, though one couldn't tell by looking at him. If the line behind him hadn't been so long, he'd have tried to flirt a bit, but it was, so he left the Quick Trip and continued on his way home.

If he had remembered his gloves, it would have been great, but he hadn't, so he kept one hand in his pocket and switched back and forth frequently. The door to the apartment was propped open. His roommate's girlfriend, whom he hated but who was super hot, was applying black and gold face paint to her man. Her name was Kristen. She didn't like sports or really anything, except Rob. She was a theater major, so she knew a thing or two about makeup and had also volunteered to drive them to the game. Two of her friends were there, too; they were less hot, but nice. He sort of liked the blonde, but there was no time for any of that nonsense now. He put the beer in the refrigerator and grabbed one for himself.

There was a fierce game of foosball going on. He quickly put the backpack in his room and returned. His "Boys" were already a few beers ahead and, as such, were screaming "Go Hawks" after each goal. The nice girls were watching and pretending to be impressed. Somebody asked for predictions for the final score, a few people yelled out numbers, the neighbors from next door popped in for a minute. Someone had heard of an after-hours party at a fraternity and post-game bar choices were discussed.

He grabbed a piece of pizza, yelled "Pan, Pan," and was met with approving grunts from the roommates. Rob's girlfriend aggressively rolled her eyes. The nice ones giggled. He started talking with them, but his mind was on the game. The nice girls were going on about something in their art history classes; he threw out something about liking the "Hudson River School" and then let them ramble on.

He had only missed one home game this year, against OSU, and the general consensus was that the majority of the blame fell on his shoulders. He had pointed out that he was good luck for the

Hawkeyes, and that they should respect his power and possibly pay homage through gifts of beer. This had been going on for weeks. There were attempts at serious discussions about Iowa's chances, but they quickly dissolved into "blowout." He agreed.

"No face paint," he said, and pointed out that he had never worn it to any of the previous games and that it would bring bad luck. The rest of the guys weren't buying it, and twenty minutes later, his entire torso and face were covered in black and gold. He looked in the mirror. It wasn't so bad, and he had to admit that Rob's evil girlfriend had done a good job.

She dropped them off at Carver. They had had plenty of time for liquid enthusiasm and were ready. Up the stairs, past the guy who was always scalping tickets. There were usually a few guys, but the guy named Brian had a phone and was more reliable than the others. They had their tickets and just said, "Go Hawks" in lieu of a greeting.

They were among the early arrivals. The seats had just a smattering of people sitting in them. His friends went to their seats; he went to the restroom. He had just eaten pizza, but an additional hot dog had never hurt anyone, and it wasn't crowded yet. He ate it and stood along the railing at the top of all the seats. It was part of his routine. He would always spend a few minutes scanning the arena and taking it all in before heading down the steps to their seats near the front. They weren't in the first row, but they were close enough that an errant pass could end up in his hands. He had gotten his hands on a ball during the

Brigham Young game and made a nice bounce pass back to the ref. From his spot, he could see his friends, standing and talking to a few fans who sat near them.

The Hawkeyes ran out for warm ups. It was time to take his seat, or at the very least, stand in front of it. He was on the aisle and took off his coat. The suggestion from Rob that he should go shirtless to the game, sans coat either, was rejected, but now that he was inside, the coat and shirt came off with a war cry. High fives were issued. He was already feeling like he was in game mode.

It would be a tough game if the first game had been any indication. He watched Roy shooting and tried to help him focus. This was another routine. Each game, during warm-ups, he would stare at one player and try to will him to a good game. It worked, sometimes. This was too important of a game to leave to chance. Once he felt that Roy had been given a sufficient amount of luck for the game, he turned his attention to the Illini side. Tony Wysinger had had 34 points in the first game. If he could send some negative vibes his way, he was sure he could shave 20 points off his performance. Miss it...Miss it...Miss it... Oh, he did, and a layup, too. Miss it... Somebody asked him if he wanted anything from concessions. He shook his head, but didn't break his focus on Wysinger. After a few minutes, he was sure Tony was going to have a miserable game and possibly become so depressed that he would quit the game and become a florist. He chuckled to himself.

It was getting close to game time, and that always made him feel giddy. The players left the floor and returned to the locker rooms. The next time out, they would have the introductions and then it would be game time. He'd make sure to give Tony another dose of the evil eye before the tip. The stands were filling up quickly now. With nothing else left to do, he found his favorite cheerleader and watched her do some back flips. She was impressive. He had seen her downtown before, but had never talked to her. He imagined that if he did, she would immediately fall deeply in love with him, and well, he her. But that would probably ruin his focus for the rest of the home games and be far too costly for the Hawks, so he kept his distance.

The band started playing "In Heaven There is No Beer" as he and his friends sang. After the post song cheering, the band went into the Iowa Fight song. They were ready. Let the game begin.

******

The old adage about the glass being half full or half empty could easily be applied to sports, especially basketball. To the fan, having your team overcome a 22-point deficit to win is a great comeback, while the opposing team's supporters are bandying about words like "choke." It's always boiled down to these two camps. For Illinois, the loss by 3 at home on January 14 was still the thing of nightmares, and there was a bit of bad blood between Ken Norman and Ed Horton. It was reported in the Chicago Sun-Times that a fight had nearly happened between the two. Norman was unhappy because he said Horton had elbowed him in the eye.

The recipe certainly seemed like one that might have led to tears for the Hawkeyes. Carver Hawkeye Arena was sold out. Despite the recent setbacks, Iowa was still ranked fourth in the nation and facing an equally impressive eleventh-ranked Illini squad.

The press about the bad feelings led to a battle of a game, or, in other words, a typical Big Ten contest. Roy Marble was asked about the play. "It was a very physical game because of the publicity about bad feelings between the teams," he said. "I just tried to play above any of the rough stuff and leave it to the referees to call. ... That's what coach Davis told me to do. He came to me personally and asked me to play above it, not to let any rough play bother me."

Al Lorenzen made the most of his playing time, grabbing 5 rebounds and scoring 6 points in his 10 minutes of play. He said of his performance: "At least we didn't fall behind by 22 points as we did in our first game against Illinois at Champagne. I just wanted to take advantage of the opportunity to play today and contribute something. I've got to keep the pressure on."

The game, being watched coast to coast, reached the first television timeout with Illinois in the lead 12–6. The game stayed even after that until the Hawkeyes went on one of their runs. With the score favoring Illinois 25–21, Iowa outpaced Illinois by a 16–2 margin and led 37–27. Carver Hawkeye Arena was rocking. Illinois added 4 more before half and Iowa added 2, so the score stood 39–31 at the break.

The Fighting Illini came out for the second half determined. Altenberger and Wysinger each nailed three-pointers as part of a 10-point run to start the half. The score was Illinois 41–39. From that point in the game it remained close. Illinois finished with a slight rebounding edge 37–34, but also committed many more fouls, leading to 33 free throw attempts for Iowa and only 7 for Illinois. Iowa also did a better job of taking care of the ball, having only 7 turnovers, compared to the Illini with 13.

It was a battle right down to the end. With only 1:23 remaining, Tony Wysinger drained a three-point bucket to give Illinois the lead, 61–60. The next trip down the floor for Iowa found Lohaus with the ball and a path to the basket for an easy 2. There was nothing Lowell Hamilton could do; he had to foul. This sent Brad to the line with a chance to tie or take the lead. He chose the latter, making them both. The clock showed only 59 seconds remained.

A missed opportunity by Illinois, and Lohaus had the ball, which forced Ken Norman to intentionally foul him. Lohaus was clutch that night and made them both, giving Iowa a three-point lead, 64–61, with a scant 24 seconds remaining.

Coach Lou Henson called an Illinois timeout, with 21 seconds remaining, to set up a three-point play. When play resumed, Illinois got the ball in the hands of Altenberger, who was shooting over 52 percent from beyond the three-point line for the year. He missed. With 6 seconds remaining, Illinois fouled Brad Lohaus again. He made them both, and Iowa won 66–61.

For the night, Lohaus led all Iowa scorers with 13, while Marble, Wright, and Moe each had 10.

Tom Davis was asked about a tough decision he had to make when choosing who would start. Ed Horton and Kevin Gamble had shown up late for a 7:30 a.m. practice, and Davis decided they wouldn't be able to start against Illinois. It is one thing to have integrity; it is another to have it when facing the number eleven-ranked team in the nation. Dr. Tom Davis made the call, the right call, and sat them. In their place, Jeff Moe and Gerry Wright started. Davis said, "I didn't feel comfortable with it, but it was something we had to do. It came at a bad time for Eddie and Kevin, but it's one of those things and it's over."

The leading scorer for Illinois was Ken Norman with 18, followed by Altenberger with 17. Tony Wysinger, who had 34 in their first meeting, was held to 12. Norman was asked about the differences between the two games. "We got a little tougher on the boards than we did in the other game. Yes, I scored only two points in the second half, but I had the same shots. I just missed them." Norman had shot 7 of 9 in the first half, but cooled to 1-of-8 in the second.

Jeff Moe made a good observation when he said, "Illinois got ahead in the second half when B.J. Armstrong was out. He's our leader and our best ball handler. When he was able to get back in there, it made a big difference."

It was a good win, but their next opponent was the team that had ended the streak: Ohio State University.

Twenty Nine

Ohio State: Iowa Record (22–3)

The Buckeyes had ended the Hawkeye winning streak in their own house, nonetheless. The sting of the first loss could still be felt by both the fans and the players. Unlike the second Illinois game, where they were the team being hunted to heal a wound, this game was their chance at redemption.

Roy was ready, though anxious, like a caged cat waiting to be fed. He thought about Dennis Hopson, the senior forward for Ohio State who had lit up the Hawkeyes for 36 in their first meeting. Hopson was averaging 29 points per game for the Buckeyes. Roy didn't want to see Dennis have another big game. It ate at him, the last game, and Roy knew there was only one way to stop the acidic burning in the pit of his soul, and that was to beat Hopson and the Buckeyes.

The coaches put together tapes of the opponents, and it was up to the players to study them. Roy spent a lot of time watching tapes. It was no different than getting homework for class. It had to be done, or he would suffer. Roy certainly knew they were watching tapes of him. If he didn't put in the work in practice, he wouldn't play well in the games. If he didn't put in the work studying the opponents, then he wouldn't know what their weaknesses and tendencies were, and it would cost him points.

Roy was a studying machine. He would stare at the TV looking for patterns like whether a player favored one hand over the other when dribbling, or whether they always left their spot when someone drove the lane. These little clues became subconscious alarms that would start ringing when in the game. Everything would be going 90 mph, but the preparation would suddenly kick in and Roy would see it, the opening that was about to happen. He would drive to the spot, take the pass, and score. It slowed the game down for him.

Roy and his team stepped onto the court at St. John Arena to a packed house of enthusiastic Buckeye fans. It was sold out. Ohio State, after going on the road and beating the number one-ranked Hawkeyes, had dropped their next two to Illinois and Purdue. Their record in the Big Ten was 8–5 going into the game, and they seemed determined to add another notch to the win column.

The first half was a battle, but Roy was on fire. He shot 9-of-10 from the field for 18 of Iowa's 48 points. They led 48–47 at the break. The second half was just as close as the first. It came down to a couple of free throw shots at the end. With 30 seconds left to play, Kevin Gamble took the ball out of bounds; the pass-in didn't find a Hawkeye but wound up in Jay Burton's hands. The game was tied at 80. Ohio State called time out.

After the time out, Jerry Francis sent the ball into Burson, who quickly made for the basket; he was fouled to prevent the easy 2. An 81 percent free throw shooter, he would have two chances to put the Buckeyes on top, with only 15 seconds remaining on the clock. He missed the first. Now the pressure was really on, and the second one bounced off the iron and Gerry Wright pulled down the rebound.

The Buckeyes played tough defense, hoping to hold Iowa from scoring and to send it into overtime. The ball was passed to Gamble, who didn't have a shot with only 9 seconds remaining. He passed the ball. A few seconds later, he found his spot, got the pass, and didn't blink as he nailed it to give Iowa the lead, 82–80.

Burson had one last shot, a three-pointer, to break the hearts of the Hawkeye fans again, but missed. Iowa had just won their 23rd game, tying the mark set by the team who went to the 1980 Final Four.

Coach Williams said, "I was really pleased with the way we played tonight. I thought we did everything right in the last 5 minutes. ... Jerry Francis made a great pass to Jay, and we got what we wanted there. It was a great feeling to see our team play like that against a great Iowa team. But I don't accept moral victories or anything like that. It's a loss in a game we could have won."

When asked about playing his former assistant of seven years, Davis said, "It's a tough thing to play him. I tried to downplay that before the game, but it is tough. I wasn't exactly jumping up and down with joy after the game."

Thirty

Assembly Hall is where Hoosier fans go to cheer on Bobby Knight and his players. They used to go to Galdstein Fieldhouse, which allowed around 9,000 fans clad in Crimson and Cream, to enjoy the games, but in 1971, a new palace was opened. On December 1, 1971, Assembly Hall was opened and held 16,666 fans, but was expanded to 16,746 in 1973. In 1976, the school added seats to bring the capacity to 17,357, and 17,343 people came out to see the rematch of Indiana vs. Iowa.

Since the loss to Iowa, 88–101, the Hoosiers had run off eight consecutive Big Ten wins and were comfortably perched atop the conference standings. The Hoosier fans wanted to see the streak continue, but they REALLY wanted redemption. Indiana warmed up and went through the routine that had helped it climb the polls to the number two ranking in the nation.

Iowa went through its routine, too. They needed the win to keep in the chase for the Big Ten title, but they knew that Indiana hadn't lost at home all year. Sadly, this would not be their day.

Steve Alford, coming off three lackluster games, needed to end his slump, and he did. The Indiana rebounding was much improved, too. In the first meeting, Iowa dominated the boards, 49–19, but only managed a slight rebounding edge 39–37 in this game. In the end, it was a combination of a lot of factors—good play, good coaching, and loud fans—that led to the win, 84–75. It wasn't as close as the score let on.

Indiana jumped out to a 24–15 lead and then turned it up a notch. Quickly thereafter, it became a 34–21 game and then another run, and it was 41–23. At the half, the margin was 19, and Indiana led 46–27.

The second half saw Indiana push the margin to 23 before Roy Marble went on a tear to try to bring Iowa back, scoring 13 points, including 3 three-pointers in the final 6 minutes. Still, it only partially closed the gap, and Indiana won 84–75. Marble led all Iowa scorers with 20, while Lohaus added 16, and Moe accounted for 13 points.

The slump for Steve Alford was shown the door. He was 8 for 15, including 4-for-4 from the free throw line, scoring 24 on the night. In the previous three games, he had shot 15-for-52. Bobby Knight said, of Alford's recent woes, "We had to play through those three games with Steve going 15-for-52. This team, I don't think, could have done that the last two years."

Alford was asked if he was worried during the downturn. "Nah, Randy Wittman called me last night and said he went 7-for-37 at one stretch here. He was a pretty good shooter. If he can go through a slump, I can obviously go into a slump."

Roy gave credit where it was due, saying afterwards, "Today was like a championship game. Their guys came in and played a great game. They didn't make any mistakes. They were making their shots, and we weren't."

There is no use dwelling on what is done and Davis said, "We have 23 wins, and we are going to try for number 24. I'm just worried about Michigan State Thursday. We want to get as many "W"s as we can."

Though the score wasn't the outcome they had hoped for, there was a little good news for the Iowa fans. Dr. Tom Davis was named the District 5 coach of the year by the Basketball Writers Association. The association also honored Brad Lohaus, Roy Marble, and Roy's buddy from Flint and ISU, Jeff Grayer, by naming them to the All District Team. It didn't change the fact that they had lost the game, but it spoke of how well they had done thus far.

******

When Roy was in the second grade, he started playing basketball at the Neighborhood Men's Club. After a few years of playing, one day his coach, Mr. Franklin, sent him home. He said he had used up his eligibility. The kids playing all started in fourth grade, but Roy had started in second grade and was now in fifth grade, and the coach didn't think he should still be playing at the club. From that point on, his coaches made sure he always had a team that could challenge his skills.

Thirty One

Every program has unsung heroes that allow for everything to run smoothly. It may seem like a simple thing, but every detail must be tended to, so that the coaches and players can focus on winning.

The team who keep the gears oiled and working are Ron Fairchild, equipment manager; Del Gehrke, who manages the facility; Dave Johnston, team physician; Mike Naughton, ticket manager; John Streif, trainer and travel coordinator; Jerry Strom, administrative assistant; Dickie VanMeter, merchandising coordinator; Jim White, promotion director; and George White, the sports information director.

They may not get much more than a mention in the program, but they are vital. Without them, Carver Hawkeye Arena would not run at all. Carver Hawkeye Arena is named for Roy J. Carver, an Iowan who was very successful and donated $9.2 million to the university. Yes, the generosity of the Hawkeye supporters must also be mentioned because without them, there wouldn't be an arena for Del Gehrke to manage. Carver Hawkeye Arena replaced the Fieldhouse, which was the home of Iowa basketball for fifty-six years.

The press area is melded into the arena seating and can accommodate one hundred members of the press. It is where reporters like Mike Hlas watch and write about the games, bringing the action to those who were not able to catch the game themselves. The oval-shaped seating area begins at ground level and then descends underground, such that the arena, when viewed from outside, appears to be a simple one-story building. It is a pleasing architectural design. But that isn't all that sits below the surface. It isn't just men's and women's basketball that compete and train at Carver. The women's gymnastics events are held there, the national powerhouse wrestling team has a 6,700-square foot practice area there, and there is a 5,200-square foot training room.

It is state-of-the-art, and tonight it will be filled with fans wanting to see Michigan State handed a loss, or more accurately, to see the Hawkeyes get their 24th win.

The ferocity with which Iowa went after the ball was astounding. They crashed the boards like a team hungry for more than a win; they were craving redemption. The Indiana loss still burned in the pit of their collective stomachs, and Michigan State was the unfortunate team that had to face their wrath. The full-court press, combined with the 56–24 rebounding edge, told the tale. When the final buzzer sounded, it was Iowa 93 and Michigan State 64.

Roy had a good game. He was an impressive 7-for-11 from the field, scored 18 points, pulled down 6 rebounds, and had 4 assists. Brad Lohaus was the real monster on the boards, though.

He had almost as many rebounds as points, 12 and 13 respectively.

The shining star, wearing green and white, was Vernon Carr, who was 12-of-19 from the field with a total of 26 points and 4 rebounds.

The Hawkeyes did two things that night—they got rid of the bad taste in their mouths from the Indiana game, and they set the single season record for wins by a Hawkeye squad at 24. The old mark was set by the 1979–80 squad, who finished with a 23–10 record. The best part was that the season wasn't over, so they had some room to push the bar even higher for future teams.

******

James Naismith once said, "I am sure that no man can derive more pleasure from money or power than I do from seeing a pair of basketball goals in some out of the way place." He invented the game of basketball in 1891. He founded the University of Kansas basketball program and was a coach who had a record of 55–60. He started it all, and since the first players learned the game from him, they have worked to advance the sport.

It isn't written anywhere that one needs to pass along what one has learned to the next generation, but they do. The players, for more than a hundred years, have fallen in love with the game and taught it to their children once their own playing days were done.

Some have gone into coaching, others have taught camps, and it is with pride that they have watched the next generation move the game forward.

On August 14, 1959, a boy was born in Lansing, Michigan, one of nine children. He grew into a man, a tall man of 6' 9" and weighing 255 pounds. He played basketball at Everett in Lansing and was given the opportunity to play in college at Michigan State University. He took it, playing for two seasons, 1977–78 and 1978–79. He had 1,059 points and 491 assists, and he shot 81.6 percent from the free throw line. He had learned a lot in his short life and was given a job in the National Basketball Association when he was drafted by the team that had moved from Minneapolis to California in 1960.

He was well liked in California and helped his team to win basketball games—lots and lots of basketball games. He played in 909 games, shot 52 percent from the field, scored 17,707 points, stole the ball 1,724 times, had 374 blocked shots, 6,559 rebounds, and made his teammates better by dishing out 10,141 assists. His name, Earvin Johnson Jr., was not used as often as the moniker he was known by, "Magic".

"Magic" Johnson not only excelled at and redefined his position, winning 3 MVP awards and 3 NBA Finals MVP awards, he was voted one of the fifty greatest players in NBA history. He inspired a generation. He inspired Roy, and they became friends.

When Roy was a freshman in high school, he met Magic Johnson at the Dr. Tucker & Magic Johnson basketball camp. It took place during the summer, and Johnson was there, helping the next generation to learn the game he loved. He wasn't the only one teaching, though. Isiah Thomas, an eleven-time All-Star and two-time NBA champion; Doc Rivers, who had one NBA ring; Dr. J, Julius Erving, whose accomplishments are too many to list; Ralph Sampson, four-time All-Star; and Mark Aguirre, who ran with Isiah on those championship teams in 1989 and 1990; some of the greatest names to have ever played the game were all in one place with one goal—to pass on what they knew.

Roy had a special "in" with the camp. His high school coach, Mose Lacy, was an integral part of running the camp and was well loved by the players who came to help. They let Roy play at night with them because Magic thought he was advanced enough that he could benefit from the extra playing time. Who wouldn't improve playing with and against the greats of the game?

It was frightening, Roy admits, because he was so young and these guys were college players; they were pros. They were very good and very big pros. Magic would make sure that Roy was on his team. Isiah Thomas was usually on their team, too. On one night, Roy got a pass from Magic, and he made a move but missed the shot. Mark Aguire started to chase Roy. Roy, being a smart kid and scared, ran. Mark continued to chase him, but eventually settled for hitting him with the ball. Later, he explained that he chased Roy because he hates losing, and if you are going to shoot it, make sure you make it. He palmed young Roy's head and Doc Rivers, Dominique Wilkins, and Isiah Thomas all laughed.

Roy got to run with the best in the world for three precious summers. He tried to emulate Magic's smile, Mark's running stance with his hands wide open, and Doc Rivers's one-handed gliding dunk. He even wore a left knee sleeve because Dr. J did, though there was nothing wrong with his leg.

A young man in Flint, Michigan, had some promise. But having promise wasn't enough. He had coaches' support and encouragement from family, friends, and some of the best to have ever played the game. That is how it works with this game. You fall in love, you listen to those who came before, and then you tell the tales to those who come after.

Thirty Two

The Michigan Wolverines, who handed the Hawkeyes their second loss of the season, were the proud owners of a streak of their own. They had won their last eight meetings with the Hawks, dating back to 1983. For the Iowa seniors, especially, they were getting rather tired of the losses to the maize and blue.

Iowa, still ranked seventh, started out looking great. They rushed out to an early 7-point lead, then gave some ground and got right back to a 7-point margin. Michigan responded with its own run of 11–2, which put them in the lead, 25–23. The nationally televised game made for some good drama. Then Iowa exploded for a three-minute flurry of defense and scoring, putting up 17 points to Michigan's 2. Iowa was scoring from long range, with B.J hitting two treys and Jeff Moe nailing one.

Only 13 minutes into the game and Iowa led 40–27. Michigan was able to get the margin down to 9, but Iowa closed out the first 20 minutes with a 7-point run. Iowa led at the half, 53–37.

The second half saw excellent play from the usual suspects in black and gold. The second half shooting percentage for the Hawks was an unbeatable 71.4 percent. The play down the stretch was dominated by Marble, who scored 10 of the last 12 for the Hawkeyes. Roy finished with 21, shooting 7-for-11 from the field and pulling down 8 rebounds, second only to the 9 grabbed by Lohaus. B.J. Armstrong had a great game, too. He made 7 of his 9 attempts from the field and finished with 18 points. The leading scorer for Iowa was Jeff Moe, who had 22 on 5-of-6 from beyond the three-point line. The entire team was hot from outside, making 7 out of 9 attempts from three-point land.

Though Michigan did its best to mount a comeback, Iowa was just too strong and won the contest 95–85.

The seniors—Brad Lohaus, Gerry Wright, and Kevin Gamble—in their final game at Carver Hawkeye Arena combined for 26 points. Michigan had success with their guard play, with Gary Grant scoring 28 points and getting 10 assists. Garde Thompson had 23 points and made 5 three-pointers. These two teams were loaded with talent, and it took a good effort on the part of the Hawks to come away with the "W".

Tom Davis said, "This is the only team we hadn't beaten, and we took some pride in that and so we wanted to beat 'em. We weren't pleased with the way we played up at Michigan. They stuck it to us up there and got a good win. That bothers you when that happens." He also had some nice things to say about Wolverine players. "That Michigan backcourt won't take a back seat to anybody."

Bill Frieder was equally kind in his assessment of the Hawkeyes. "I'd say they can make a run at it. They played well, and we knew they would. They're just awesome players. Iowa's a great team, and I told you in Ann Arbor."

When Davis was asked about Roy's performance, he said, "There's no doubt that Roy is just getting better as the season has gone on. He did a lot of team things early and now he is scoring better."

So, the losing streak to Michigan was snapped, and another win was added to the Iowa record, with at least two games to play before the NCAA tournament. At that point in the season, every win mattered, because it might be the difference between a two or a three seed, and that was the difference between playing a fourteen or fifteen. It was the time of year when one must peak, and the 95–85 win was certainly a sign that Iowa was playing well.

Thirty Three

Thursday, March 5, 1987. The Iowa Hawkeyes have two more games left, the first being at Northwestern. Now, one never wants to assume a win or take an opponent lightly, but on paper, it looked pretty good for Iowa. The Wildcats had only four wins on the season and but one in the Big Ten. In the two teams' first meeting, Iowa had cruised to a 36-point win, 80–44.

The Wildcats gave a great effort and kept it close at the half, only trailing 40–50, but Iowa's long-range attack was what did it in. In the first half, Iowa made all six attempts from beyond the three-point line and finished the night 9-for-12. In the end, it was Iowa coming out on top, 103–76.

Though the game was easily won by the Hawkeyes, there were still some interesting stories, the best being the recent shooting of guard Jeff Moe. In his previous 39 attempts from behind the three-point line, he had hit 26 of them. If one were doing the math at home, then one would have seen that to accomplish the same scoring from inside the line, he would have had to have made 100 percent of his shots. In short, he had become a perfect scoring machine. Jeff Moe made 5-of-6 from three-point land, a kingdom where he had grown quite comfortable. His total points for the night was 20, which was one less than Kevin Gamble's.

Gamble had a great night. He scored 21, with 7-of-14 from the field and 6-of-7 from the free throw line. But that wasn't all he was doing. He hustled on defense and attacked the boards, pulling down 9 rebounds. He said after the game, "I felt like I've been in a slump the last five or six games. I wanted to come out and do things right. I was working on my power moves. I really went to the boards tonight, too."

Davis agreed. "Kevin Gamble has not played well since the Arizona game. To see him come back to his true form tonight—I thought that was a good sign for our ballclub."

That night the starters saw less time than usual, which meant the bench got more game action. Players like Mark Jewell, Mike Morgan, and Les Jepsen all saw 5 minutes, while Michael Reeves had seven. It was a good game for the whole team, and now the single season record stood at 26 wins.

Tom Davis was rewarded for his record-breaking year by being named the United Press International "Coach of the Year." The win against Northwestern was the 300th of his career.

Thirty Four

The regular season was one game from completion. Iowa had a chance to earn its 27th win. Fans and players alike were confident in their chances.

Sports are often used as a metaphor for life. We are taught that it is important to pass the ball and to be unselfish, which is a great life lesson. A person who spends a life in selfish pursuits is living a shallow existence that can barely be called a life. He is miserable and doesn't understand how people can be happy. The ones who give back, in part because they have learned how satisfying it is to share, are much happier overall.

Coach Davis built a team around unselfish play. The Hawkeyes became a family who cheered for and encouraged each other along the way, and that was the big key to their success.

Sports have always been a great source of motivation. The energy one gains from watching excellence motivates and inspires one to reach for greater heights. Sports and the people who play them have always provided words of encouragement for those who seek it.

"Show me a guy who's afraid to look bad, and I'll show you a guy you can beat every time."—Lou Brock

"If you can't accept losing, you can't win." —Vince Lombardi

"Nobody who ever gave his best regretted it." —George Halas

"Don't let what you can't do interfere with what you can do."
—John Wooden

If one is looking for inspiration, one doesn't need to go much
beyond the words of the players to find it. The players who gave
their all through a lifetime of dedication, sweat, and learning,
have earned the right to be heard. They have been through the
fires and faced the uncertainty of making a team, achieving a
goal, or winning a game—knowing that to lose would devastate
their worlds. And yet, they persevered.

Basketball is special because, although it is a game anyone can
play, it is easy to appreciate the difficulty in playing it well. When
we watch a baseball game, we see the batter strike out, and it
looks so easy to hit that ball, we think we could do it. We have
delusions of grandeur as fans. It is the same in football, where it
is easy to jeer the dropped pass from our couch without the
prospect of an angry linebacker thundering toward us. But
basketball is different because for most of us, we can stand under
a basket, ball in hand, and jump up and have gravity pull us back
down to earth well before the glorious dunk we imagine in our
minds. If we swing the bat, and a Hall of Fame pitcher is sending
a 98 mile-per-hour fast ball towards us, the bat and ball might,
through sheer coincidence, arrive at the same spot at the same
instant. In basketball, however, gravity is a constant, as is the fact

that most will never dunk a ball. Because of that, we see the game through a truer lens.

Sports not only motivate us to try harder, they may also give us the inspiration to overcome a fear. Failure is a miserable thing, and as such, the fear of failure is a powerful foe. Through sports, however, we can learn that although we may fail, we may still feel pride in our effort. If one matches up against a superior opponent and performs beyond their expectations, if they rise to the level of their opponent, they may realize that although they lost, they are better than they imagined. The next opponent may be within their means, and that victory will be sweet.

When we read simple words, like those of Francis Bacon, Sr.: "There is no comparison between that which is lost by not succeeding and that which is lost by not trying," it makes us realize how important it is to replace the fear of losing with a fear of not playing at all.

And so the last game of the Big Ten season arrived. The months of practice, hours of film work, pain of the battles, cold of the ice tubs, and wisdoms of the coaches were nearing an end. There were no more improvements to be made. The team was what it was and would head into the NCAA tournament on a high note or a sour one—that was the prize. Play for that one win because a loss might linger.

The ball was tipped, and Iowa came out of the shoot on fire. They quickly built a 13–3 lead on an 11–0 run. Wisconsin didn't pack it in, though, and by the time the first 20 minutes had wound off the clock, it was a close game, Iowa 42–37. The second half saw the Badgers pull within two, but Iowa never gave up the lead and kept them at bay until the end, winning 81–71.

Wisconsin finished the year with a 4–14 Big Ten record, while Iowa had the opposite result at 14–4.

Davis admitted that he had some concerns. "I was very worried about this game. I just felt if you watched around the country in what's been happening, you could see some teams that have had good years coming up with bombs at the end of the season. In our league, we've seen a couple instances like that.

"I was very worried about my ball club kind of flattening out, because we were not sure this game would have any bearing on where we'd go or play. We thought it was possible our fate was sealed when we beat Northwestern Thursday and we'd had 26 wins."

The Big Ten title was shared by Purdue and Indiana, who each had 15–3 marks in the conference. Davis said of his team's third place finish, "If you had told me a couple of weeks ago that we'd win fourteen games and would have been out of the race, I think I would not have believed it. It's a great tribute to Purdue and Indiana that they were able to get through this year with only three losses."

Roy spoke about the game, too, and said, "I was definitely worried about this game. No one wants to lose in front of their parents and this was Parents Day for their seniors. They played real hard." Marble put up good numbers, with 20 points and 5 assists.

Wisconsin coach Yoder said, "I don't think we played as well as we have been playing, but I think Iowa had a lot to do with that. Our only shortcomings today were because of Iowa, not ourselves. ... They're just a strong club. I think they're going to do well in the tournament."

Lohaus also had another great game, scoring 16 points and pulling down 8 rebounds. There were five Hawkeyes in double figures, and it was apparent that this team was ready for the NCAA tournament to begin.

*****

There are times between practices and games when Roy just sits and thinks. Remembering his life before Iowa, when he was running with T. Greene and Glen Rice, and they were called the "Flintstones", helps him stay centered.

It wasn't just their friendship that mattered, it was the fact that all three of them had strong mothers. The support and love they received helped them make good decisions when the opportunity to go astray presented itself.

For some reason, the trip he and T. took to D.C. pops into his head. They were brash, bordering on cocky, when they walked into legendary coach John Thompson's office. The coach tossed them a ball and said to dribble it. It was flat. It took the air out of their attitudes, immediately. They both got the point—basketball is fleeting; life isn't.

Going to a new city, a different team, at a higher level of competition is a frightening thing. If it weren't for Roy's "Flintstone" buddies, it would have been tough to make it. Sometimes a guy needs to have a buddy who knows what the life is like to call, to talk to, to not feel so alone. It is a hard world, Division I basketball, and everyone is working their butts off to beat you. Without friendship, it is damn near impossible to survive. T. Greene once said, "Friendship is Free," but that doesn't mean it isn't valuable. It is the most precious thing one can have.

Roy remembers how all three of them fought like rabid dogs on the court, but the moment the game was over, they were best friends again. They always knew that there were two worlds—basketball and life. If you let them mix, it would be tough to excel at either.

Roy's break was over. He had taken a moment to focus on all that was important off the court. If there was a minute, later in the day, he might give T. a call. For the moment, however, he had to get ready for class.

Thirty Five

NCAA Tournament: Selection Sunday

It was the best month of the year, March. Ask any sports fan, and they'll tell you that it is the month that teams gather across the country to crown a national champion. Before they do, though, the teams are chosen by the selection committee.

A group of basketball gurus comes down from its secret basketball lair atop Mount Naismith carrying its magical books where they are able to see all that happens across the hardwood of our great nation. There are automatic qualifiers who earn their way by winning their conference championships, and the rest are selected or rejected on merit.

Part of the magic of March is the teams who win their way in. Sometimes it is a team who has had a miserable season because of injury, bad luck, or just not being as good as its opponents, but the players put it all together for a weekend and do the unthinkable—they win. They sneak past their first opponent because they are underestimated, and then they rise to their second round challenge and slay their foe. Now they are in the finals and everyone knows, on any given day, if the shots fall, they get to play for it all.

Those teams are often very low seeds, but they are dangerous because they have nothing to lose. Do the guys who play for the Gonzagas of the world work less hard than those at Kentucky?

No. They started in the same driveways, ran just as many suicides in high school, and have the same love of the game; they just went to smaller schools. Admittedly, the blue chippers go to the Big Ten, Big Eight, Big East, SEC, and conferences of the like, but it doesn't mean the little guy can't win. They can, they do, and it is what makes the tournament special.

So, the committee gathers and they pick. Across the country, teams gather for a meal. Some teams— Iowa, UNLV, Indiana, and the others who have spent most of the season near the top of the charts—aren't worried about being selected. They still worry, though, because it isn't just making the tournament that counts, it is the seed. A number one seed will play a sixteen the first round. In the history of the tournament, a one has never lost to a sixteen. The two seed plays the fifteen, and so on and so forth. There is also the matter of where one will play. The closer a game is to the school, the easier it will be for the faithful to make the trip. And the last vital bit of news is who a team will play. This bit is most important to the coach because the chances are pretty good he won't have seen a single game of his opponent or have any film on it. His team will have, at most, three days to prepare, and the coach knows better than anyone that upsets happen, especially in March.

There is the other end of the spectrum, too. The teams that make the tournament will likely be first round cannon fodder for the higher seeds. They wait, they worry, but their concerns are only one: Will they make it? There is a name for these teams; they are "on the Bubble", and it is a painful place to be. They gather and wait for the announcement of the brackets. With every new pairing announced, there are cheers, somewhere, and two fewer spots for the bubble teams. They wait, they pray, and if their ticket remains unpunched, they take solace in a probable invite to the N.I.T.

Thirty Six

The advantage to being one of the top teams in the country is the high ranking and subsequent first round game against a lower seed. Iowa, a two seed, faced fifteenth seed Santa Clara. Santa Clara had last been to the "Big Dance" in 1970, under coach Dick Garibaldi. Now, under the guidance of Carroll Williams, it would face the Hawkeyes.

Santa Clara had some great teams in the past. From 1952–54, it made it to the National Semifinals, Elite Eight twice. Still, Iowa was the better team and should have been able to handle them.

Iowa took the game seriously, which is a key to avoiding an embarrassing upset. Santa Clara struggled mightily. It was a great game to watch, if you were a Hawkeye fan, had a heart condition, and needed to avoid stress. Santa Clara scored the first 4 points of the game and then only had one more field goal in the first 15 minutes of the first half. Iowa threw in a 22–0 run and the die was cast.

The starters for Iowa watched the last 15 minutes of the game from the bench. Roy Marble played 22 minutes, the most of any starter. He had 16 points on 8-of-10 shooting from the field. The leading scorer for the Hawks was Kevin Gamble. He was 8-for-8, and 2-of-2 from the free throw line.

The real hero of the game was the Iowa full-court pressure. During their run, they forced 7 turnovers. Brad Moody, who played 17 minutes for Santa Clara, said, "I don't think it was so much our nervousness. They hit us with pressure, we had some turnovers, we got flustered and from that point it was difficult to bounce back."

Coach Carol Williams summed up the game: "Iowa obviously felt sorry for us and took the pressure off. We've faced a number of different presses but you just don't simulate Iowa's in practice. We panicked and had too many turnovers and were never in the flow. It is easy to summarize the game. They beat us in every phase."

The bright light for Santa Clara was Jens Gordon, who played 37 minutes and scored 24 on 9-of-14 shooting, had 6 rebounds, and made all 6 of his free throw attempts.

The final score was 99–76. Fourteen players saw at least 5 minutes of action for the Hawkeyes, and everyone scored. It was Iowa's 28th win of the year.

Thirty Seven

UTEP: Iowa Record (28-4)

The field starts with sixty-four teams spread across sixteen sites around the U.S. March Madness is in full swing once the first game tips on Thursday morning. Brackets have been filled out, copies made, ducats put into a jar, and pride laid on the line—and that is just for the fans. For the players it is called "The Big Dance," mostly because once they are selected and then with each stop along the way, all one wants to do is dance.

Iowa has outlasted thirty-two teams and now faces the University of Texas at El Paso, in Tucson, Arizona. Ask anyone who has ever filled out a bracket and watched teams they've never heard of knock off a team they thought would advance to the Sweet Sixteen, Elite Eight, or Final Four about upsets, and they will explain how it is anybody's game when March rolls around. There is an interesting dynamic from the fans who attend the games. When one buys tickets for the first rounds, they are actually getting seats for the first two games and then the single game of the second round. Everyone cheers for his team, but everyone seems to cheer for the underdog in the other games. If a twelve seed wins, they will very likely have the "Cinderella Story Fans" on their side, yelling and screaming to see the unlikely underdogs advance to the Sweet Sixteen.

UTEP isn't a stranger to the NCAA tournament. In fact, it has something Iowa doesn't. It has a National Championship and not just any championship, either, but one of the most famous in history. The school was known by the name Texas Western Miners in 1966, and it shocked the world by playing a style of basketball not seen before, with players—and also not seen before—who weren't white. Adolph Rupp, the legendary coach from Kentucky, took a dim view of the "colored" player and was beaten 72–65 by Bobby Hill and the Miners. It changed the game forever, and for the better.

Now, it's time to play the second round.

The tip goes to UTEP as Tim Hardaway gets control. He passes the ball to Chris Sandle, who, with toes on the three-point line, sinks the long bucket. The Miners get back on defense as Iowa pushes the ball up court. Brad Lohaus takes the first shot for Iowa, missing a three-pointer, and UTEP is off to the races. They quickly get the ball to the other end, but an ill-advised shot down low ends up heading out of bounds, and Iowa gets it back.

Iowa's first basket comes down low with an easy basket, and the score is tied at 2. Both teams are battling back and forth; it is going to be a fast-paced game. Roy makes a nice move in the lane and scores. He then immediately sneaks back to intercept the inbounds pass and lays it in for two more, and Iowa leads 6–2.

UTEP is a team that doesn't mess around on the offensive end, putting up the shots quickly, and Iowa is doing a good job of controlling the boards. A rebound, by Iowa, pushed to the other end, and a shot is missed. Tim Hardaway gets the ball and takes it coast to coast to bring the score to 6–4, Iowa. The crowd definitely seems to be cheering for the upset.

Iowa scores and then after some more tough play, finds itself with the ball out of bounds on the offensive end of the floor. UTEP steals this inbounds pass, and Jackson sprints to the other end and lays it in. This UTEP team loves to run. The score is 8–6 Iowa.

Lohaus misses, UTEP runs to the other end, a pass is made, and the shot is missed. Iowa sprints back to the other end, and Jones turns it over. Everyone needs to run the other way. Jeff Moe makes a smart foul to stop the 3-on-1 break, and UTEP gets the ball out of bounds. It gives Iowa a chance to set up its defense. UTEP slows it up for a moment, makes a couple of passes, and then Sandle hits again from right on the three-point line.

At the other end, Jeff Moe, whose toes never get near the three-point line, drains a long jumper. This puts Iowa up by 5. Steve Jackson answers with his own three-pointer, and now the score shows Iowa leading 13–11.

It doesn't look like a two-versus-fifteen matchup. The Miners are matching Iowa in skill and intensity, but will it last? The Iowa bench is much deeper, and Dr. Tom Davis has been making more substitutions than Haskins.

All this running, shooting, and amazing basketball has only taken 5 minutes off the clock. The fans in Tucson are getting their money's worth.

Iowa, running a rather slow possession by this game's standards, sees Tim Hardaway steal the ball. The Hawkeyes sprint back on defense, and Hardaway chooses not to sprint to the other end. Instead, he makes a three-quarter court pass, and Chris Blocker fires up an uncontested shot and makes it. The game is tied.

Iowa gets a little careless with the ball, and Keith Jackson is quick to the other end to lay it up for two and the first lead since being up 2–0. UTEP 15–13.

The running continues, and UTEP stays up, leading 19–17, but then Gerry Wright sees Marble running to the basket and throws up a beautiful alleyoop pass, which Roy has no qualms about dunking. It is tied, again.

A quick shot, but off the mark, hits only the backboard, and Iowa is able to get the rebound and jump out to a four-on-one break despite the UTEP players running full speed to catch up. It is truly a blistering pace. The problem for Iowa is that the one person back is Hardaway. His quick hands intercept the pass, and he is immediately running the other way. It happens so quickly that nobody on the Iowa team can recover, and he throws down an easy dunk.

Iowa tries to set up but has another turnover. The crowd, with the exception of the Iowa fans, is loving it. For a fifteen seed to be running with such a talented two, well, that is why they call it "March Madness." The big story thus far has been the turnovers. Iowa has given it up nine times compared to UTEP's four.

Marble scores for his eighth point of the game, but UTEP comes out running and catches Iowa not getting back quickly enough, and the Miners score on a 3-on-1 break and get fouled. Jackson misses his free throw, but Campbell is there for the rebound and bucket. UTEP leads 25–23.

Nine minutes remain in the first half, and Horton is fouled and makes only the front end. The game stays close as both sides maintain a high level of defensive energy. Every basket is contested, and the fouls are adding up. Both teams are getting turnovers, the clock is running, and with only 6:30 remaining, Iowa ties the game at 28.

Marble, after a good defensive stop by the Hawkeyes, pulls up and hits his fifth of five attempts for a total of 10 points in the game. UTEP scores and then Marble gets a tip in for his twelfth point of the night, and he is still perfect from the field. Iowa leads 32–30.

Neither team has been able to pull away from the other, and the score at the half is UTEP in the lead 42– 38.

The second half begins, and UTEP expands the lead to five, 44–39, but Gamble quickly scores, and it is back to three points. Both teams have led by five.

The offenses explode for both teams, and they exchange buckets for several minutes, with almost every trip down the floor resulting in some points. With just over 4 minutes gone, the score has ballooned to 52–51. The Miners and the Hawkeyes are firing on all cylinders.

Just as quickly, the defenses of both teams take over, and the next 3 minutes see much less scoring. Lohaus sinks a three-pointer to put Iowa up 57–56, with twelve to play in regulation. Ninety seconds later, after two UTEP buckets, Lohaus strikes again from long range. His second three-pointer ties it at 60.

A three-pointer and a fast break bucket give UTEP a 65–60 lead, and Iowa calls a time out with 9:23 left to play.

As the clock winds under 8 minutes, a basket by Gates, for UTEP, pushes the lead to 69–62. The Iowa fans are starting to get a little bit nervous. They have seen their beloved Hawkeyes come back over and over again, but how many times will they be able to go to that well?

It is B.J. Armstrong who answers the black and gold-clad prayers with a three-pointer from the corner. A short while later, after a couple of baskets, Marble takes an inbounds pass and scores. It is his 22nd point, and Iowa is only trailing by two, 71–69. With 5 minutes remaining, Roy Marble steps to the line and makes two free throws. The game is tied at 71, the tenth time the scores have been equal.

UTEP earns the lead back with a bucket, but on the ensuing trip down the floor, Mark Jewell gets his fifth foul and is out of the game. Kevin Gamble makes both free throws, and the score is 73 all.

UTEP brings it up and quickly shoots a three-pointer, which misses, and Ed Horton pulls down the board. Iowa pushes it to the other end, and the clock hits the 4-minute mark. Lohaus is fouled trying to give Iowa the lead. He makes the second one, and Iowa leads 74–73.

Richmond gets a chance to return the favor, but only manages to make one of two himself, and the game is tied again.

With less than 3 minutes to play, Roy Marble is sent to the line, and he makes them both. Iowa leads 76–74, Lohaus grabs the rebound on UTEP's next possession, and B.J. brings it up court. All the fans seem to be standing, regardless of the team they are cheering for. Horton makes a high arching pass to Gamble, who is in perfect position down low and makes the easy layup. Iowa 78–74.

Richmond answers with a bucket and the foul. He makes it, and it is a one-point game with less than 2 minutes to play. Dr. Tom Davis calls a time out. Afterwards, Iowa calmly looks for the shot, and Marble sees an opening. He puts it up, but it kicks off the iron and heads towards the out of bounds. Ed Horton jumps in the air, retrieves the ball from landing out, and throws a high lob pass out to Armstrong. Iowa gets a new shot clock with 1:35 remaining.

With just over a minute to play, Marble passes to Horton, who takes it up strong and scores. Iowa leads 80–77. A shot by Hardaway at the other end is short, and Iowa gathers up the rebound. With only 32 seconds remaining, Davis calls a time out. The Hawkeye band strikes up the Iowa fight song.

On the inbounds pass, after the time out, Roy is fouled immediately. He makes the first one to make it a two-possession game. He makes the second, and it is 82–77, Iowa.

UTEP gets two points with 9 seconds remaining.

After a time out, Lohaus takes a play from Chuck Long's playbook and hits Gary Wright with a beautiful pass. "Sir Jamalot" throws it down and is fouled. He makes it. Hardaway adds a three at the buzzer, and Iowa advances to the "Sweet Sixteen" with an 85–82 victory.

Thirty Eight

Oklahoma: Iowa Record (29-4)

The Oklahoma Sooners, a six seed, had to tough it out against Tulsa, winning 74–68 in the first game. Their next game was even tougher, beating Pittsburgh 96–93. Now, they prepare to take on the Hawkeyes for a chance to be one of the last eight teams standing.

It will be a battle of similar defensive styles. Both Billy Tubbs, the Oklahoma coach, and Dr. Tom Davis rely on it to wear their teams down. And if each team is trying to wear down the other, the game may be decided by the depth of the bench.

The players are announced. The coaches, Dr. Tom Davis and Billy Tubs, exchange warm handshakes and smiles. The fans in Seattle are ready, as are the ones back in Iowa and Oklahoma. It is time to get this game underway. Iowa starts the familiar five: Lohaus, Marble, Wright, Armstrong, and Gamble. For Oklahoma: David Johnson, Daryl Kennedy, Harvey Grant, Ricky Grace, and Tim McCallister will take the floor.

Billy Tubs says before the game that he doesn't like playing teams that slow the pace down. "If they slow it down, I just won't guard them." He doesn't need to worry about Iowa; they like to run.

Iowa controls the tip as B.J. Armstrong gets the ball in the back court. Armstrong over to Wright, who gives it right back. Oklahoma is playing a tight man-to-man defense, and Iowa is moving well without the ball, cutting and screening, looking for the high percentage play. Marble gets the ball and drives into the lane, takes it up, but is blocked.

Grant gets the rebound off the blocked shot and brings up the floor. Davis has Iowa playing a man-to-man defense, too. The Sooners work the ball into Grant, and the Iowa defenders collapse on him in the lane. He shuffles his feet and is called for traveling.

At the other end, the Sooners aren't giving Iowa any good looks at the basket. The Hawkeyes pass the ball around the outside, looking for an opportunity. Lohaus passes to Marble, and then he sends back to Lohaus. Now, Wright, Gamble, and Armstrong rotate outside and control the ball as Marble and Lohaus run the baseline. The movement without the ball is making Oklahoma expend a lot of energy to cover the Hawks. It continues until the ball is nearly stolen, but Gamble recovers it. He passes to Armstrong out near center court, and Ricky Grace is right there with him. Finally, with the clock winding down, Armstrong is forced to put up a shot and misses.

Ricky Grace runs down a long outlet pass. It is too strong for him to be able to lay up the ball without stopping. He recovers deep under the basket and is fouled while taking it up. It is Roy Marble's first. Grace looks comfortable at the line and has been shooting 70 percent from the charity stripe. He makes the first one. The second one is good, too. Oklahoma leads 2–0.

Oklahoma applies their full-court pressure, and Iowa handles it well. They get the ball across the time-line and try to send it into Marble, but the ball is picked off by the Sooner. They quickly run to the other end, finding David Johnson on the left side about twelve feet from the basket. He makes the shot look easy and Oklahoma is in front, 4–0.

Two Sooners look to trap Armstrong in the back court, but he uses a burst of speed and zips past them. He takes it all the way into the lane, jumps, shoots, and is fouled by Grace. The arc on the shot is like something from a basketball textbook and the cheerleaders yell, "Whomp" as he swishes the first shot. The second is as pretty as the first, and Iowa has its first points of the game.

The Sooners get the ball out to the wing on the right side, and Gerry Wright is right on the shooter, McCallister. A lob pass inside and then it is kicked right back out after Wright collapses on the man down low. McCallister shoots and hits the three-pointer.

At the other end, Gamble takes it inside along the baseline and is fouled by McCallister. Gamble misses the first free throw and then the second, but Marble skies and pulls down the rebound and is fouled by the 6'9" junior from Sparta, Georgia, Harvey Grant. Lohaus takes the ball out under the basket. He passes it in and then gets the ball right back. It gets knocked out of his hands, and soon there are bodies diving for the ball. It eventually squirts out, and McCallister picks it up off the floor.

At the other end, they slow it up and let the rest of the Sooners get caught up with the action. Grant posts up and takes the pass; he turns and fires a jumper, but misses. Armstrong pulls down the rebound and is off to the races. He takes it all the way to the hoop, draws the defenders, and drops it off to Gamble, who gets an easy bucket.

Oklahoma handles the trap and gets the ball over the time-line. It's a 3-on-2 break, and Grant gets the shot, good. Oklahoma leads 9–4. On the other end, the possession for Iowa yields nothing, and the Sooners are running again.

McCallister takes a long three from the wing and misses, but Johnson gets the rebound and then takes a quick shot. He misses, too. Gerry Wright is in perfect position and grabs the board. He gives the ball to Armstrong, who sprints across the line and sends a long pass to Gamble in the corner. Gamble puts the ball on the floor and then elevates for a routine jumper. Iowa trails, 6–9.

The action on Oklahoma's end of the floor is intense. Guys are banging, and eventually the ball is knocked out of bounds, off Iowa. Jeff Moe comes off the bench for Iowa. The play resumes, and the Sooners put up a shot from the left side. It bounces out to the right, and McCallister gets the rebound. He pulls it outside, and they reset their offense. Iowa's defense is making it hard to score, but Oklahoma's rebounding is keeping it in their hands. Eventually David Johnson travels and turns the ball over to Iowa.

Horton on the wing gets the ball. He drives across the lane and is fouled before he can shoot. It is David Johnson's first foul of the contest. Al Lorenzen checks in for Lohaus and takes the ball out under the Iowa basket. He sends a bounce pass in, but it is picked off. A 2-on-1 break ensues and ends with a thundering Harvey Grant dunk. The assist goes to Ricky Grace. Grant was fouled on the play, so he goes to the line to try to complete the three-point play. Harvey Grant, whose twin brother, Horace, plays for Clemson, makes the free throw. Oklahoma leads 12–6 in an exciting West Regional game.

Jeff Moe takes a quick three-point try, and Al Lorenzen is called for an over-the-back foul while trying to grab the rebound. Oklahoma takes the ball out of bounds and quickly gets it in Grant's hands at the other end. He makes a routine turnaround baseline jumper.

At the other end, Al Lorenzen weaves his way through the defenders in the paint and lays it in. Oklahoma gets it to the other end almost immediately, and McCallister gets fouled by Horton while going for a reverse layup. McCallister misses the first one from the line. The second one is too strong, and Marble pulls down the board.

At the other end, Moe misses his second three-point attempt and Oklahoma gets the ball. Hustling back, Moe dives for the ball and knocks it out of bounds, stopping a 2-on-1 break and a likely easy two points. At the first television timeout, it is Oklahoma leading 14–8, with 14:12 remaining in the half.

Both teams are playing up-tempo ball. Of the 27 possessions thus far, only two—and both by Iowa—ran more than 25 seconds off the shot clock. Oklahoma's Ricky Grace puts up a fifteen-foot jumper from just to the right of the free throw line, and it's good. Oklahoma doubles up Iowa, 16–8.

Getting their offense set quickly, Jeff Moe finds his spot in the corner, takes the three-pointer and makes it. Oklahoma responds with two points from Daryl Kennedy. Both teams seem to have found their offense. Iowa gets the ball in the paint, and Wright takes it up, but it won't fall. Gamble has perfect position for the rebound; he grabs it and goes back up immediately, scoring easily.

Iowa immediately puts on the pressure with the full-court press. Oklahoma gets it in, but just barely, then Iowa traps. The Sooners barely escape, and Iowa falls back across mid-court and sets up its defense. Just under 12:00 remain in the half. Despite its best efforts, Oklahoma sends in a perfect jump pass to Grant, who makes an un-defendable jump hook. Iowa tries to force it inside, but it is for naught. Oklahoma ball and they are running to the other end.

Grace takes a long three, which results in a long rebound. The Sooners kick it back outside. They try an alleyoop pass, looking for an easy dunk, but Lohaus denies it. The ball goes out of bounds off Oklahoma.

Iowa shows some poise on offense, not rushing it, like the last trip, and then Wright sees the smallest of openings. He makes a brilliant spin move past his defender and scores. The Iowa faithful are on their feet. They are silenced a few seconds later when two long passes gets the ball to Kennedy, who is able to put it in with an easy shot just outside the paint.

B.J. takes it coast to coast to make the score 22–16, Oklahoma. The Sooners answer with another bucket. Both teams are on fire. B.J tries going the length of the court, again, but is fouled. He makes both free throws to keep Iowa within 6.

Harvey Grant has found his range and nails another shot. He has 10 points on 5-of-6 shooting from the floor.

Iowa, still aggressive on the offensive end, gets the ball stolen, and Ricky Grace takes it all the way to the hole for an easy bucket. Oklahoma leads 28–18, their largest lead of the game.

Armstrong takes a shot, and Lorenzen grabs the rebound. He dribbles once and gets the ball knocked away. Oklahoma comes away with it. They take a quick shot but miss, and Iowa grabs the rebound. Everyone sprints back the other way. It just doesn't look good for the Hawkeyes right now. They seem out of rhythm and aren't living up to their ranking. Of course, this is a team that has been down before, and often, and its signature move has been to come back, again and again. Still, the fans nibbling on sliders and drinking a beer or two at George's in Iowa City would rather they get things going, sooner than later. Iowa turns it over with a foul on Lorenzen.

Oklahoma takes advantage with a three-pointer by McCallister from the left side. Oklahoma 31–18, is threatening to run Iowa out of the gym. At the other end, Grant blocks the shot, and Oklahoma is running once more. Stacy King tries to sink a floater, but it is too strong, and the rebound is grabbed by Iowa. Play is stopped. Gerry Wright has been called for a foul.

Iowa sends the ball into Horton, who gets his pocket picked. Oklahoma ball and quickly turns it into two points, but King is called for a foul after the shot. Horton will shoot the one-and-one. He makes them both, erasing the damage from the steal. Oklahoma leads 33–20 with 8:13 remaining in the half.

Grant misses a turnaround jumper but gets his own rebound and makes his second shot.

B.J brings the ball up court and calls the play. He takes it to the right side, and Jeff Moe rotates to the top of the key. Armstrong to Moe and quickly over to Marble, but Moe is fouled by McCallister. Moe makes the first one but misses the second. The ball goes out of bounds and is given to the Sooners.

Oklahoma quickly breaks the press and gets the ball into McCallister's hands on the wing. He elevates and makes the shot to give the Sooners a 37–21 lead.

Iowa, still playing hard, gets the ball to Marble, who is fouled driving the lane. Marble sends up the first free throw. It bounces twice on the front of the rim and then slides into the basket. It is his first point of the game. He has averaged 22 points through the first two games. The second one is good, too.

Oklahoma shows some patience and passes the ball around looking for the shot. After a handful of passes, Iowa gets a hand on the ball and steals it. B.J. pushes the tempo and misses the shot, but Horton grabs the rebound and takes it up strong—good.

The Sooners inbounds with a baseball pass all the way to the other end. McCallister takes the long two-point shot before anyone can get in his face. He misses, and the long rebound goes to Iowa, who immediately gets it in B.J.'s hands. Oklahoma tries to trap him, but he squeezes between them and dribbles back into open court near the top of the key. B.J. gives it off to Moe, who sees a sliver of an opening and makes a perfect bounce pass into Horton. He takes it up strong and Iowa has scored 6 unanswered points.

Iowa steals another long baseball pass and is on the attack again. Marble dishes to Lohaus, but it is picked off. Oklahoma gets a 3-on-1 break, and B.J. takes a charge from 6'7" senior David Johnson. Iowa is doing everything right to get back into this game.

Just under 6 minutes before the break, Moe sends it to Lorenzen, who passes it and then rotates. The ball is back to Moe at the top of the key, and he works it around to the right. A pass inside to Horton, he shoots, but it's blocked. The ball sails into Moe's hands just outside the three-point arc. He doesn't hesitate and sends up the shot. It is in and out. Oklahoma gets the rebound.

At the other end, Oklahoma is sent to the line but misses the front end. Johnson grabs the rebound and puts it up, but misses. Another rebound for the Sooners, but Iowa quickly traps. The ball gets knocked out of bounds off a Hawkeye leg. Gerry Wright comes back into the game. After the inbounds pass, the ball is swung around the outside until McCallister puts up a long three attempt. Wright grabs the rebound and sends an outlet pass to a sprinting. He is all alone ahead of the pack and take the layup. Goal tending is called, and Iowa gets the bucket. Oklahoma leads 37–29 as Iowa plays its way back into the game. Just over 5 minutes remain in the half.

Iowa switches to a man-to-man defense. They get the ball inside, and Lorenzen does a good job on his man, number 33, King. The shot is too strong, and David Johnson gets the rebound on the other side of the court. He sends it back to the top of the key. A pass inside is deflected out of bounds.

Iowa, who usually dominates on the glass has been out rebounded 20–12. Oklahoma brings the ball in and immediately gets it inside to Ricky Grace, who puts up a shot. Michael Reaves gets the board for Iowa and pushes the ball up the floor. Oklahoma isn't giving anything away inside and eventually tips the ball out of bounds. Lohaus to inbound. B.J. takes the pass and brings it to the middle. Lohaus finds a spot down low and gets a nice pass, but is unable to convert. Marble called for a foul during the rebound. It is Stacy King at the line shooting the front end of the one-and-one. He misses, and Marble gets the rebound.

Iowa works the ball around and eventually Gamble gets a good look at the basket and makes it. The lead is cut to six, 37–31.

Oklahoma gets the ball inside, but Lohaus blocks the shot and Gerry Wright comes away with the rebound. Lohaus, yet to score, puts up a three-pointer. It is off the mark, but Wright grabs the board and takes it back up for two. It's a four-point game.

At the other end of the court, Oklahoma, on a bit of a drought, gets called for the charge; turnover, Iowa ball. More importantly, it is the third foul on Ricky Grace, which could put the Sooners in a tough spot. Grace heads to the bench. It is Marble at the line. The first one hits nothing but net. He misses the second, Iowa puts it back up, blocked, but Gamble gets it and goes strong to the hole. He misses, and Lohaus tips the ball to himself. He dishes it out to Wright, who has an open fifteen footer, but gives a head fake and goes around his man. The twelve-footer is good. Iowa trails by one.

The Iowa bench is on its feet with only a touch over 2 minutes remaining in the half. Daryl Kennedy is called for a foul, and B.J. will head to the line for a one-and-one. Armstrong ties the game with the first one. A deep breath and three bounces later, B.J. makes the second free throw, and Iowa takes the lead 38–37. An amazing comeback, and this is why they call it "March Madness."

Dave Sieger gives it to David Johnson, who sends up an errant turnaround jumper. Brad Lohaus is all over the glass and gets the rebound. He passes it to B.J., who then sends it into Moe in the corner. Oklahoma, respecting his long-range shot, has two men in his face. Moe passes and rotates outside. He gets the ball back near the top of the key and fires, but it is just a touch too strong. Tim McCallister, the 6' 3" guard from Gary, Indiana, gets the board. The clock shows 1:42 until intermission.

Oklahoma moves the ball around. They have been cold and are looking for an inside bucket. They dump it down low, and Armstrong fouls to prevent the score. Iowa has scored 17 unanswered points. David Johnson misses his first attempt. The second is no better, and the carom goes out of bounds—Iowa ball. 1:18 remaining in the half.

Jeff Moe puts up a shot, which is off the mark. The ball sails out of bounds, and after the referees confer, it is determined, correctly, that it was last touched by Iowa.

Oklahoma sticking to its quick shooting philosophy misses a three, and Iowa is running the other way. Horton to Lohaus down low. He has position, head fakes, and takes it up for his first bucket of the game. Iowa leads, 40–37.

With 32 seconds remaining in the half, Oklahoma scores its first points in over 7 minutes and trails by one, 39–40. Iowa is holding the ball for the last shot. Oklahoma goes for a steal on a bounce pass but just knocks it out of bounds. The Sooners steal the inbounds pass with 15 seconds left. Johnson scores underneath and the Sooners lead again, 41–40. The final four ticks run off the clock.

Halftime

Oklahoma's Rickey Grace starts things off in the second half. He passes to McCallister, who has his shot blocked. B.J. runs down the ball before it goes out and makes a nice dribble behind the back as he brings it up court. A perfect pass to Gamble, and he banks it off the glass.

Iowa playing zone forces Oklahoma to keep the ball outside, and McCallister doesn't mind. He hits a three-pointer from the top of the key. The Sooners back in front.

Iowa gets the ball down low, and several shots and rebounds later, Gamble finally gets the bucket. The game is tied at 44. B.J. steals the ball at the other end and takes off with his teammates in stride. He makes a perfect leading bounce pass to Gerry Wright, aka "Sir Jamalot," who elevates and throws down a monster dunk. He is called for a charge, but the basket is counted.

David Johnson answers with a turn-around jumper at the other end, and the score is 46 apiece.

Lohaus, who has been having a rough night, sends up a three-pointer and gets a "Shooters roll," giving Iowa the lead, 49–46.

At the Oklahoma end of the floor, the ball is worked inside to Grant, who goes up for the shot and is fouled. It is Brad Lohaus who is called for the foul, Iowa's second of the half and his first of the game. Grant makes his 14th and 15th points by sinking both free throws.

Iowa has an unproductive trip down the floor, ending in a travel. David Johnson makes a tough shot over Lohaus. B.J. gets the inbounds pass and takes it all the way to the other end, where he stops and nails a jumper to put Iowa back in front 51–50.

McCallister lobs the ball inside, and it is immediately kicked back out to him. He is set beyond the three-point line and strokes in the trey.

Iowa loses the ball after a half dozen passes. Grace with the steal, passes to McCallister, who finds Johnson in the lane. Johnson shoots and scores. Oklahoma builds its lead to four.

Iowa keeps the ball outside, but before they can get a good look, Kennedy is called for a hold. Lohaus and Wright are replaced by Moe and Lorenzen. A lob pass into Horton, and he goes up with the shot. It bounces to Lorenzen, who takes it back up, but misses and is fouled by Grant. It is his third. Al Lorenzen, a 53 percent free throw shooter, makes them both.

The Sooner three attempt misses, and Iowa brings it up with B.J. leading the charge. Al Lorenzen is spotted up fifteen feet from the basket, unguarded, and B.J. sends him a chest-high pass. He makes the jump shot look easy. It is all tied up at 55. There is

15:21 remaining on the clock to decide who will move on to the "Elite Eight."

Oklahoma breaks the press, and two long passes get them to the other end. Iowa is back on defense and stops the rush, so they kick it back out. Eventually, they find Johnson, who is surrounded by three Hawkeyes. He still manages to make a jump shot, and the Sooners are back up by two.

Iowa almost throws the ball away, but a hustling Jeff Moe saves it to Lorenzen. The Hawks look for the inside shot, rotate, and work the ball into Lorenzen down low. He takes it up and scores.

At the other end, McCallister eyes the long two, but the defender makes him think otherwise. He passes it back to Grace. A poor shot, then a rebound, by Grant. He goes up but can't connect, and Horton grabs the board.

B.J. jumps like he is going to shoot, but instead passes it to Moe, who instantly sends it in to Horton. Horton turns and fires, but it is short. Lorenzen darts to the glass and gets the board. He is fouled, by Grace, his fourth, and Lorenzen will head to the line. Dave Sieger checks in for Oklahoma, and Harvey Grace heads to the bench. Lorenzen makes them both and has 10 points off the bench. Iowa leads 59– 57, but over 13 minutes remain on the clock. It is still anybody's game.

Oklahoma gets through the full-court press and Iowa hustles back on defense. Iowa is keeping everything out of the paint. They are going to force the outside shot, and McCallister obliges. The long three-pointer misses and kicks off the rim and out of bounds.

Iowa tries to work it inside, but their efforts are thwarted and the Sooners take it away. They set up and look for an opening to take the ball inside. Lorenzen gets called for a foul. It is his third of the game. Oklahoma gets the ball in with a long pass and then sends it inside to Grant. He goes up for the shot, but it is no good. Dave Sieger is there for the put back, and the game is tied at 59. Grant gets called for his fourth foul during the play, but the basket counts.

Iowa gets its offense set and works the ball around to Gamble, who drives across the lane and makes the bucket. The inbounds pass is tipped to Lohaus, who turns and fires off the glass, but it doesn't fall. Oklahoma comes away with the ball. Johnson gets good position, is fed the ball, and tries a turnaround jumper, but he's fouled by Wright. He'll shoot two.

Johnson misses both shots, but the Sooners come away with the rebound. They reset their offense and pass the ball around until Kennedy gets it in the corner. He makes the long two. It is 61 all with less than 11 minutes remaining in regulation.

Lohaus drives in and draws the defenders. He dishes off to Marble, who tries a difficult shot, which is no good, but Lohaus is there for the tip-in.

On the inbounds pass, Iowa again causes problems, and McCallister knocks it out of bounds, but the referees say it is Oklahoma ball. A smattering of boos rain down from the Hawkeye fans. Oklahoma is having trouble getting the ball in to play and calls a time-out before a five-second violation is called.

They have no trouble getting the ball in after the time-out. The Sooners bring it up the floor, and Tim McCallister makes a three-pointer, to give Oklahoma the lead, 64–63.

At the other end, Marble answers with a baseline jumper, and Iowa is back in front, 65–64. Marble hustles back on defense and almost gets a steal under the basket, but the referee says the ball touched out of bounds. Oklahoma makes a long lob pass to get the ball in play, and McCallister quickly puts up and makes another three.

Marble gets the ball down low and takes it up strong. He is fouled but makes the bucket. He will go to the line for a chance to convert the three-point play. It is Darly Kennedy's third personal foul and Oklahoma, who has only gone seven deep on its bench, is getting in foul trouble. Marble misses the free throw, and Oklahoma grabs the rebound and immediately pushes it up the floor. David Johnson gets the ball and takes it up strong to give the Sooners a 69–67 lead.

Gamble wastes no time getting the ball to the rack, but is fouled and will go to the line. Every trip down the floor that results in an Oklahoma foul is a bonus for the Hawks, as they have a much deeper bench. Gamble misses the first, but swishes the second, and the lead is cut to one.

Another near steal for Iowa, but the Sooners make it across the time-line. A bullet pass underneath to Kennedy, and he takes it up strong for the score.

Gamble is again attacking the paint. He drives across the lane and fires up a shot, it is good, and he is fouled. Daryl Kennedy is credited with the foul and now has four. Gamble makes the shot from the line, and the game is tied.

Oklahoma moves the ball around the perimeter, the clock ticks down to 8:30, and Iowa tries to prevent the inside shot. McCallister settles for a three-point attempt from the top of the key, but it is short, and the hard carom is grabbed by the Hawkeyes. An outlet pass is made to Marble, who is well ahead of any Oklahoma defenders, and he dunks it with ease. The Iowa fans are on their feet.

Oklahoma tries to get a quick bucket, but Horton stops play with a foul. The Sooners pass the ball in. They pass it to Kennedy, who kicks it to McCallister, who double pumps and takes it up and is fouled by Gamble. McCallister hits the back of the iron on the first free throw but drains the second one to give him 23 on the day.

Gamble, again, takes the ball on the left side, dribbles across the lane, jumps, and shoots. It is a move that the Sooners have not found an answer for, and he makes it again. Iowa leads 75–72 with just under 8 minutes left in the second half.

The Sooners set up, Sieger thinks about a shot from the top of the key but passes instead. They move the ball around and then try to force it inside. Roy Marble comes up with the steal. He rushes to the other end but sees that Oklahoma is back, and he pulls up. B.J. now with the ball. B.J. directs the offense, and Iowa scores.

The clock continues to run, as do both teams, and at the 6:32 mark, Oklahoma makes a three to bring the score to Iowa 78 and Oklahoma 76.

Iowa continues to play controlled when they have the ball. Oklahoma, looking a little fatigued, is making great effort on defense. Tim McCallister almost comes up with a steal but kicks the ball out of bounds. Harvey Grant, with 4 fouls, checks back into the game for Watson.

Iowa, despite more than a dozen passes, just can't get the bucket. 5:44 remains, and McCallister brings the ball up to the foul line, elevates, and shoots. No good, but Daryl Kennedy gets the rebound, and there aren't any Hawkeyes to prevent him from making an easy reverse dunk. The game is tied at 78.

Iowa again misses on the offensive end. Kennedy gets a good look from just past the free throw line, but it doesn't go in. Gerry

Wright gets called for a foul on the rebound attempt. Iowa is over the foul limit, and David Johnson heads to the line and makes them both with ease. Oklahoma leads 80–78.

After the TV timeout, Iowa again works the ball around the outside. A quick pass into Roy Marble, and he elevates for the shot, but Lohaus is open underneath, and he dumps it off. Lohaus puts it up and in.

The Sooners answer with a basket and with a shade over 3 minutes remaining, Oklahoma leading 82-80.

Ed Horton is called for a foul on Iowa's next trip down the floor. Dave Sieger will shoot the one-and-one for the Sooners. He makes the first, misses the second, but in the ensuing battle for the rebound, the ball is knocked out of bounds by Iowa.

Oklahoma pushes the lead to 85–80, but with just over 2 minutes remaining, the Hawkeyes defense steps up. Marble hits a shot with 2:04 remaining, and the defense refuses to let Oklahoma score. B.J. nails a three-pointer to tie it, and only 51 seconds remain. Neither team would score again in regulation.

Iowa opens the overtime with two points from Gerry Wright at the free throw line. The defense holds, and then B.J. sinks a three-pointer. Iowa leads, and the fans in Black and Gold are going wild. They are silenced by a 6-point Oklahoma run, giving the Sooners the lead, 91–90.

Kevin Gamble, who has been a steady source of points for the Hawkeyes, and has made 10-of-12 from the field, for 19 points, gets the ball. Time is running out, and he takes his second three-point shot of the game. Iowa fans across the state, the country, and especially in Seattle, hold their collective breath. It is good! Iowa takes the lead 93–91.

The last second heave by Oklahoma misses, and the Hawkeyes have won their thirtieth game of the year.

Thirty Nine

In Seattle, Washington, site of the West Regional Finals, two teams get ready to come out for their Sweet Sixteen game. Every man in the locker room has the same feeling in his gut. It is one born of the knowledge that their season continues only if they win. The tournament is down to five teams. Everyone else has gone home and is watching the games on TV. Those players are wishing they were where the University of Nevada Las Vegas and Iowa are right now—on CBS, about to get introduced.

The country has already watched Syracuse beat North Carolina, Providence get past Georgetown, and Indiana top LSU. All that remains is this last game to fill out the Final Four bracket. The winner of this game gets to face Indiana.

The announcer calls the line-ups and they are ready to play. Iowa starts Brad Lohaus, Roy Marble, Gerry Wright, B.J. Armstrong, and Kevin Gamble, while the Running Rebels send out Gerald Paddioa, Armon Gilliam, Jarvis Basnight, Mark Wade, and Freddie Banks. The Hawkeyes and Running Rebels have met only once, in 1978, and UNLV got the win 85–84.

The tip goes to Freddie Banks. He doesn't bother waiting for his team to catch up; he fires and misses the opening shot of the game. The ball bounces high off the iron, and Banks is able to run down his shot. UNLV sets up its offense. Two passes around the perimeter and Gerald Paddioa takes a three-pointer from the left side but misses. The ball goes off a UNLV player and is out of bounds. The referee signals that the ball belongs to Iowa.

UNLV starts with a pressure defense, but Lohaus gets the ball into B.J. with little effort. A screen near mid-court helps B.J. bring the ball across the center line. He passes it to Lohaus at the top of the key, who passes it left, but the ball comes right back to him. Brad then swings it over to Wright, who sends it along to Gamble. Gamble sees that Roy has position and makes a nice bounce pass to him. Wright breaks for the basket; Marble makes a fake jump shot, draws the defender, and drops the ball off to Wright, who scores the first bucket of the game.

Iowa sets up its defense and it isn't as aggressive a press as they have used most of the season. UNLV brings the ball up the floor. Mark Wade tries a baseball pass, which is fielded by Wright. Wright turns around and makes a hard overhand pass to B.J., and the Hawks are running the other way. B.J. looks like he is going to shoot, but finds Marble underneath. The ball rolls off the rim and a blur of dunking Lohaus flies in and jams it home. Iowa takes the early lea 4–0. They are now in their familiar full-court press.

UNLV, obviously well prepared, gets the ball in and moves it up court. Wade sends the ball over to Freddie Banks on the left, who has no qualms about firing up a three-pointer. It's good and now a one-point game.

Iowa brings it up court quickly and moves the ball rapidly around the perimeter. Marble is battling for position underneath as Lohaus and the others are all around the three-point line. B.J. puts up a three, and Lohaus gets the rebound. He is fouled going up for a shot. The 7'-senior calmly dribbles the ball, studies the rim, and then puts up a perfect swish. The second shot is equally impressive, and Iowa leads 6–3.

UNLV breaks the press and gets out ahead of Iowa, leading to an easy dunk for Gerald Paddioa. There is a reason they are called the "Running Rebels."

Iowa sets up their offense again. The UNLV defense is aggressive and forces a travel. The Rebels take advantage, work the ball inside, and Jarvis Basnight gets a dunk off the missed shot. UNLV takes its first lead, 7–6.

At the other end, Iowa continues to move the ball and look for the passing lanes. Gerry Wright finds Lohaus, who takes it up strong. The UNLV defender gets a massive palm on the ball from behind, and Brad pulls the ball through and puts up a nice layup. It is hard to believe the ball didn't get stolen or knocked out of his hands. Iowa back in front, 8–7.

UNLV almost fumbles away the inbounds pass, but quick feet gather the ball back up. They work the ball into Gilliam, who has to shoot to over the Lohaus, who quickly gets his feet set and arms up. The ball bounces off the rim and is pulled down by Gamble, who is out running immediately. B.J. is running, too, and takes position near the top of the key. Gamble dishes the ball off to B.J., who drains a smooth jump shot. Considering what is on the line, a ticket to the Final Four, all ten men on the floor are playing with great poise and energy. It is a fun game to watch.

Iowa's press yields a steal by Gamble, who sinks an eight-foot jumper, giving Iowa the 12–7 lead.

On the other end, Gamble hustles and tries to pick Armon Gilliam's pocket, but hits his arm and is called for a reach-in foul. UNLV inbounds and before anyone on either team is set-up, a pass and a shot. It misses, and Gilliam gets called for over-the-back on Lohaus.

UNLV gets a bit more aggressive with its full-court press, but B.J. patiently works the ball back and forth until he is over the ten-second line. Armstrong passes it to Wright, who sends Lohaus, but Basnight is there and almost gets the steal. Lohaus regains control of the ball and gives it back to Wright, who takes the jumper and makes it. Iowa leads 14–7, but there is a lot of game left to play.

UNLV, who has been struggling from the floor, gets the ball into Gilliam. He puts up the shot, but it caroms off the back of the iron. He grabs the rebound and tries again, this time making it. The Running Rebels' fans come to life.

Al Lorenzen and Ed Horton enter the game. The trainers take a look at Lohaus, who is sporting a black eye from practice that required ten stitches. The Big Ten is brutal, both in the game and during practice. B.J. brings the ball up and sees that UNLV isn't moving its feet, and he turns on a burst of speed and nails a shot from the paint.

Freddie Banks gets the ball at the top of the key and puts up a jumper with a little too much juice. The rebound is pulled down by Marble, who quickly gets it out to his buddy B.J., who gets it right back to him. The UNLV defense is set, and Roy gets rung up for a charge. Davis gives Gamble a breather and sends in Jeff Moe. Also entering the game for Iowa is Michael Reaves.

UNLV fires up a long three-pointer, misses, gathers the rebound, shoots again, and misses again, but gets the board. Another quick shot, which also comes off the iron hot, and finally Iowa comes away with the rebound.

Iowa takes little time in setting up its offense. They players pass the ball around, and the Running Rebels lose track of Michael Reaves, who gets the pass under the boards, then fakes, and—after the defender sails past—lays it in.

The first television time-out arrives with 14:26 left in the half, and Iowa is out in front 18–9. The sponsors get their say, and then we return to the action. UNLV with the ball, seems to only be looking to shoot from outside, and on this trip it pays off with a three-pointer from Mark Wade. He is not a frequent shooter for the Rebels, and Iowa plays a touch soft on defense when he gets the ball.

Iowa has a bad possession, getting called for a five-second violation and gives the ball back to UNLV. Jeff Moe gets called for a foul on the inbounds pass.

Banks shoots, misses, and gets his own rebound. He takes it up strong and comes crashing to the floor. Gilliam gets the rebound and tries to take it up but is fouled by Moe. UNLV ball under the basket. Iowa plays its typical tight inbounds defense and almost gets the steal when Ed Horton and Gilliam both get their hands on the ball. Gilliam wrestles the ball away and puts up a shot, making it and closing the gap.

Iowa works the ball around the outside and then Lorenzen makes a great pass to Gamble, who is fouled by Gilliam in the act of shooting. Gamble, coming off an 11-of-13 shooting night in their Sweet Sixteen game against Oklahoma, steps to the line. He makes the first one. The second shot is better looking than the first. He makes it, and the Hawks immediately begin to press. Iowa leads by 4, 20–16.

Wade brings the ball across mid-court, showing little concern for the pressure defense. The Rebels work the ball around until Gilliam is in position. He turns and puts up a shot, making it easily. It's a two-point game.

Armstrong takes the inbounds pass and sprints up the floor. He makes a nice pass but is fouled, stopping play. Jerry Tarkanian calls time-out with 12:16 seconds left in the half. During the time-out, the referees conferred at the scorer's table, and it was determined that UNLV had been given an extra basket, so they adjusted the score to 20–16, Iowa. With as fast as the action has been, who could blame them? It is all sorted, and Iowa takes the ball out.

UNLV is upping the adrenaline on its defense and trying to trap. Iowa has handled it thus far, but there have been a couple passes nearly picked-off. Iowa tries to get the ball inside, but the defenders quickly collapse, and the ball is kicked back out. Eventually all the hard work by the Rebels pays off, and they get the steal they've been looking for, along the baseline.

The UNLV possession ends with a quick shot and a rebound by Marble. Iowa sets up its defense, and then Hudson grabs Marble and tries to throw him to the ground. He is called for the foul, his composure having left him in the heat of the battle. Marble doesn't react and just walks away. He would give his answer with a spectacular reverse layup, get fouled, and go to the line for a shot at a three-point play. Marble puts up the free throw. It bounces twice on the rim, trying to make up its mind about going in, but just as it seems to be leaning towards "no," Lohaus tips it in for two.

Iowa tips the inbounds pass, but a Rebel comes up with it, and they head to the offensive end of the court and set up. One pass and number 32, Gary Graham, sinks a three-pointer to bring UNLV to within 5, 19–24.

Iowa moves the ball around until Wright sees an open shot. It is too strong, but Marble pulls down the board, and Iowa resets its offense. B.J., from the top of the key, moves to his right, passes to Wright, who is looking to send the ball inside. Everyone is covered, so he passes back to Lohaus, who sends it over to B.J., and they continue to look for inside points. B.J. sends it back to Lohaus, who finds Gamble. Gamble makes a nice dribble move into the lane and sinks the shot. His speed wins the day, as nobody was close to blocking the attempt.

Armon Gilliam gets a long rebound off of a missed three attempt and puts it up and in to make the score 26–21, Iowa.

Iowa takes a play from the Rebels playbook and immediately fires up a shot before the defenders are able to get set. It hasn't worked well for the Rebels, for the most part, and this attempt misses, too. Marble is fouled on the rebound. The front end of the one-and-one rattles out, and UNLV is fouled on the rebound by Gerry Wright, his first of the game.

UNLV misses another long-three attempt, but the resulting rebound ends up in the Rebels' hands, and they work the ball back inside. Gilliam takes the pass and makes a smooth turnaround jumper.

Iowa sets up again. Gerry Wright has it in the corner and sees a flash of B.J. Armstrong running to the basket. Wright feeds him a beautiful bounce pass, which Armstrong takes to the hole. He makes it and is fouled. B.J receives the ball from the referee and takes a big breath. He lets it out and the eyes focus on the basket, three deliberate bounces of the ball and he puts it up, but it just won't go in. UNLV gets the rebound.

Freddie Banks takes the ball on the left side of the court, thinks about a three-pointer, but fakes and drives around the defender to get an easy ten-footer. Iowa still leads, but only by 3, 28–25.

B.J. makes a long pass to Moe, it almost gets taken away, but he gets the ball and dishes it off to Marble, who makes an amazing blind pass to Wright, who takes it up and is fouled. A 50 percent free throw shooter, he misses the first one, but makes the second.

Wade forces the ball to the corner, and Graham makes a long two-pointer. Iowa remains in front, 29–27. On offense Iowa is called for a blocking foul and UNLV gets the ball back with a chance to tie or take the lead.

Wade considers the shot, but sends it to the corner to his right, and Gary Graham nails the three, giving UNLV the lead 30–29. The Running Rebels then make a nice stand on defense and get the ball back. It feels like a momentum shift, and the cheerleaders in their red and white with bow ties are going crazy.

Jeff Moe makes a great hustle play, stealing the inbounds pass, but steps on the line and turns it back over. David Willard takes the ball out for UNLV, but because it is from Jeff stepping out of bounds, isn't allowed to run the baseline. He takes a two-step and is called for travelling, thus giving the ball back to Iowa.

Lohaus gets the ball and drives the lane, but is fouled by Willard. Lohaus ties the game by making his first free throw. He makes the second one, and Iowa is back on top.

UNLV gets the ball in before Iowa can get set, and it is a sprint to the other end. Gerry Wright fouls to prevent the basket. Iowa has done a nice job from the free throw line, making 7-of-11, while UNLV hasn't had an attempt before now. Mark Wade misses his first attempt. He makes the second.

Michael Reaves gets the ball before the mid-court line and takes off like a jack rabbit, to the hole, and lays it in. He may have broken the sound barrier with that sprint. He runs back after making the shot, then turns and leaps in front of the pass to intercept the UNLV inbounds play. Michael Reaves is on fire. He passes it to Gamble, the crowed is roaring, and Gamble elevates and nails the bucket, and is fouled. Gamble takes a breath, looks calm and relaxed, and swishes the free throw.

With just under 8 minutes remaining in the first half, Iowa has a somewhat tenuous 36–31 lead. All indications are that this is going to be a battle right up to the end.

UNLV brings the ball up and then passes it to Gerry Wright, or at least, that is what it looks like. In truth, it is simply a matter of great anticipation on Wright's part as he steps into the passing lane and snatches the ball out of the air. Men in black and gold start sprinting to the other end, and the lone UNLV player under the boards, Freddie Banks, gets set and takes the charge.

Banks is helped up and then moments later, the basketball frenzy begins again. The Running Rebels fire the ball across mid-court and get the ball to Banks, who takes a look at a three-pointer, then drives the baseline, but misses. Marble goes up strong and pulls down the rebound. He is fouled. It is Jarvis Basnight who is the guilty party and it is his third.

Basnight goes to the bench and is replaced by Eldridge Hudson, number 33. Roy misses the front end, and UNLV gets the board. A couple of quick passes and then Banks takes shot from beyond the three-point line, but it is short, and Iowa's Wright pulls down the rebound. He sends the ball over to Reaves, who runs it up court and then finds Lohaus, who fires up a three. It, too, misses.

UNLV, faced with a 2-on-3 break, decides to slow it up and pulls the ball outside. A moment later Graham takes a long two but misses, and Marble grabs another rebound. He gets the ball ahead to Reaves, who then kicks it back outside, and Iowa sets up its offense. Before Iowa can get the look inside it wants, Brad Lohaus is fouled. He misses, and Hudson pulls down the board for UNLV.

Iowa, playing tight defense, forces the Running Rebels to knock the ball out of bounds. Al Lorenzen checks back in for Iowa as Davis continues to rotate in the bench to keep the legs fresh. Gerald Paddioa returns for UNLV. The score has remained unchanged for the last 2 minutes, 36–31, until Wright decides it might be a good time to send up an alleyoop for his buddy Roy Marble, who throws it down. The crowd approves noisily.

UNLV, again, takes a quick shot at the other end, and it is one and done. B.J. gets the rebound and hurries the ball over the half-court line, but before he can shoot, there is a foul away from the ball. Armstrong heads to the line and makes the first one. The second one is as good as the first. Iowa has now matched its earlier lead of nine, 40–31.

The Running Rebels seem content to drive in for one shot, and this time it is Banks who puts it up. He misses everything, and Jeff Moe is there for the air ball. Moe immediately sends it out to B.J., who is off to the races. The Rebels do a great job of hustling back and almost get a steal. Iowa settles down and tries to set up its offense, but an errant pass is picked off.

Freddie Banks misses another long-range shot. Hudson fouls Armstrong and sends him to the line. It is Hudson's third foul of the half. On the sideline, Jerry Tarkanian starts chewing on a white towel as he paces. This does nothing to stop B.J. from making both his free throws.

At the other end, Gerald Paddioa gets a good look at the basket and makes it, ending an 11–0 run by the Hawkeyes. Iowa leads 42–33.

B.J. hurries to the other end and spies Jeff Moe all alone in the corner. A brisk pass and a jump shot later, the scorer adds three to the Iowa total. Banks tries to answer with a three from beyond the NBA line used for Seattle Supersonic games, but hits the front end of the rim. Iowa is unable to get the rebound, and two quick passes later, they fire up another, but it hits and bounces over the backboard. Iowa gets the ball. It is leading the number one ranked team in the nation, 45–33, with under 5 minutes remaining in the first half.

Iowa, who has made a habit of getting the shot off in under 15 seconds this game, slows it up. They work it back and forth between B.J and Jeff and then a few more passes, and it comes right back to them. The UNLV defense isn't letting Iowa inside. Finally, Moe sends it to Lorenzen, who gives it to Marble along the right baseline. Mable makes a nice bounce pass to Ed Horton who takes it up strong and scores.

UNLV shoots quickly, and Lorenzen goes up for the rebound. It is contested by UNLV, but it is Roy Marble who pulls it down. Marble to B.J. and then he passes it to Wright on the break, who lays it in. UNLV tries a three-quarter court inbounds pass, but it is B.J who gets to it first. He brings it up and finds Moe in the corner. Moe passes it inside to Horton, who takes it up, scores, and is fouled. Iowa leads 51–33, but the Rebels aren't out of it yet. They have twice come back from major deficits, 19 and 22 points, this year. Coach Tarkanian calls a time-out.

Ed Horton stands at the line with a chance to add one to their lead but misses. He doesn't just miss, it's an air ball. Coach Davis yells his support from the sideline, and UNLV takes the ball out of bounds. Freddie Banks misses another three-pointer as the Running Rebels are now shooting 25 percent from behind the three-point line. His teammate Armon Gilliam is there for the rebound and takes it right back up for a nice jumper. Iowa 51–35.

At the other end, Ed Horton gets the bucket right back with a great shot off the glass. The Rebels get a baseball pass in to midcourt almost immediately after the Horton shot goes through the rim. It catches Iowa by surprise, but they are saved by a traveling call. The clock approaches 2:30 remaining.

On the possession, Iowa gets a touch sloppy with the ball and throws it away. UNLV again tries to make it rain from outside but comes up dry. There is a foul on the rebound, and Iowa goes to the line. It is Gary Graham's third foul. Jeff Moe puts up the first, hits the front of the iron, the ball trickles over and drops through. He adjusts but sends the second attempt long. Horton is there for the rebound and takes it to the rack, but it is blocked.

In transition, Banks makes a nice bounce pass, and Paddioa gets the layup. Iowa leads 54–37. With the clock falling below 2 minutes in the half, Iowa slows it up, looking for the good shot. A foul sends Armon Gilliam to the line for UNLV. The transfer from Independence Junior college makes only the first one.

Ninety seconds remain, and B.J. finds Gerry Wright, who sees Marble breaking for the basket. They try another alleyoop, but this time the Rebels get a hand on it, and break up the play. Lohaus, trying to grab the ball, fouls and sends Gerald Paddioa to the line. He makes them both.

Iowa again being cautious with the ball gets it in Moe's hands. UNLV tries to trap, but he fights his way through it and passes back to B.J. The ball comes back to Moe, he drives in, kicks it out to Lohaus, who makes a long cross-court pass back to B.J. Under one minute left in the half. The ball goes inside to Wright, who uses some nice touch to put it in. Iowa leads by 16, 56–40.

UNLV runs 15 seconds off the clock, an eternity by their standards, and is fouled when they try to get it inside. Gerry Wright picks up his third foul. Gilliam goes to the line and picks up his 14th and 15th points.

It looked like Iowa might try to wait for the last shot, but West fouls and puts an end to that idea. B.J. hits both free throws. The last trip down the floor yields nothing for UNLV, and Iowa leads at the break, 58–42.

Half-Time

Returning to the floor, Iowa is undefeated when leading at the half, while UNLV is also undefeated when trailing at the half. Something is going to have to give. Brad Lohaus sends the ball into B.J. to begin the second half of play. The first shot of the half goes awry, and UNLV gets it out of bounds.

The 6'-senior, Mark Wade, brings the ball up court as everyone sprints to the other end of the floor. He doesn't even look to pass, but gets his toes across the three-point line and fires it up. The rebound is pulled down by Lohaus, and he sends it over to Armstrong. As he gets across the center line, his feet get tangled up and he goes to the floor. B.J. maintains his cool and gathers the ball up and gets it to Lohaus, before the defender can tie him up, for the jump ball. Lohaus passes it over to Gamble, while Gerry Wright and Roy Marble roam the baseline.

Iowa passes the ball around looking for the opening inside. Iowa runs the shot clock down to 5 seconds and B.J. puts up a shot along the baseline, but it doesn't go in, and UNLV gets the board. Two quick passes, and Armon Gilliam is making an easy layup at the other end.

The Hawkeyes bring the ball over the half court line and immediately throw it out of bounds. It looks like a communication error. The Running Rebel fans erupt. Ed Horton checks into the game, and Gerry Wright takes a seat.

Wade brings the ball up. The Iowa full-court press isn't quite as intense as it was in the first half. Easily across the timeline, he passes it to Paddioa, who puts up a three and misses. Gamble gets the rebound and quickly moves away from the traffic. He brings the ball up, and nine other guys dash to the other end. There isn't a man on the floor who isn't giving 100 percent. Selfless effort in sports, for the good of the team, is a thing of beauty.

Gamble takes the ball to the left and then kicks it back to Armstrong, who makes a nice jumper. Iowa leads 60–44.

UNLV takes the ball out of bounds and fires a long pass up the sideline. Mark Wade, running like a gazelle, soars towards the basket. B.J Armstrong looks fearless as he takes the charge.

Iowa brings the ball up, and Mark Wade, who has just been called for charging as he drove to the basket, doesn't notice the seven-footer, Brad Lohaus, setting the pick. Wade is called for charging again. It is his fourth foul, and he is pulled from the game.

Iowa takes advantage and Gamble makes a jump shot in the paint. Iowa leads 62–44, but that quickly changes. Freddie Banks shoots a near NBA three-pointer, and the Rebels pull to within 15 points.

Off the trey, UNLV presses, and though Iowa gets the ball across the ten-second line, it doesn't come easily. Marble takes the ball baseline, but the Rebel defenders are there to knock it out of bounds. Iowa gets the ball in under the boards, but is unable to convert.

UNLV controls the ball out past the three-point line. The Iowa defenders are well off of the shooters and bunched around the lane. If UNLV is going to score, it is going to be from outside. A couple of passes back and forth, and finally they put up a long shot, which misses, but Paddioa gathers the rebound and sends it to Banks, who is spotted up a foot past the three-point arc and drains it. Iowa leads 64–55. The UNLV bench explodes with excitement.

The crowd is deafening, and the cheers are for a comeback. It seems to feed the Running Rebel defenders because they are making it hard for Iowa to run the plays they want. Moe is almost trapped but makes a nice cross-court pass, and Iowa is able to settle down. They get the ball to Roy underneath, and he misses. UNLV gets the rebound and pushes it up the floor, and B.J almost steals a pass. Banks comes away with the ball and fires up a trey, misses, but gets fouled by Jeff Moe. He makes the first and second. The lead is down to seven.

Iowa continues to run its offense, but there is still more than 13 minutes remaining. B.J. is fouled by Gary Graham, his fourth. Coach Tarkanian makes the decision to put his starter, the senior Mark Wade, back in the game. He will be playing with 4 fouls. Iowa inbounds the ball to B.J., who dribbles to the right and gets it to Wright on the wing. The defense shifts over, and he sends it back to B.J, who passes it to Lohaus on the left. They work the ball back around until a small gap allows a pass into Marble. He goes up, but misses. Lohaus is there for the rebound and put back. Iowa leads 66–57.

UNLV makes a couple of passes, looking for a good shot, and then Wade arcs a lob pass into the 6'9" Armon Gilliam, who tosses it in from five feet. The entire UNLV bench is standing and yelling encouragement. Only 12:30 remains in the game.

An attempt is made to trap B.J. in the back court, but he gets the ball over the line to Lohaus. Iowa continues to pass the ball around the outside looking for a shot. Finally, Roy is open, but misses the shot. Eldridge Hudson pulls down the rebound.

Wade to Paddioa, three-pointer, good.

Iowa's lead has been cut to four, 66–62, and the number one team in the nation is rolling. Iowa rushes the shot, and UNLV has the ball again.

Wade first up another bomb from the corner, but it is too strong. The rebound is handled by UNLV and is worked back around to Wade. A few passes later, and UNLV tries to work it inside, but the pass caroms out of bounds. It's a turnover, Iowa ball.

Graham, off to the races, gets a great look from about ten feet, but hits the front of the iron. The ball shoots straight into the waiting arms of Ed Horton, and Iowa is going the other way. Iowa moves the ball around the outside looking for a good shot. With the lead, they aren't afraid to run some clock. To the Hawk fans, both in Seattle and across Iowa, it can't move quickly enough. UNLV isn't giving an inch. With a scant 7 seconds remaining on the shot clock, Gamble nails a shot from just inside the top of the key. They burned clock and got the bucket. It was a good possession.

A few seconds later, UNLV fires up another three, and Ed Horton adds one to his rebounding total. The Hawkeye 3-on-2 break ends in a charge issued to Gamble. Jeff Moe checks into the game. The Iowa five are Reaves, Moe, Lorenzen, Horton, and Gamble. Armon Gilliam gets position on the baseline and makes the jumper. Iowa leads 64–49.

After burning some clock, Iowa is called for traveling and turns the ball over. At the other end, Paddioa shoots a three over Lorenzen and makes it. The Running Rebels are starting to heat up from outside. The lead is now 12.

Iowa, looking for a quick score, is called for a charge on Gamble. UNLV will have a chance to cut the lead to single digits. Along the sidelines, Dr. Tom Davis walks with furrowed brow. He looks up at the scoreboard, hands in pockets, and calculates his next move. He shakes his head, Kevin Gamble has just picked up his fourth; 14:58 remain in the game.

Iowa tries a lob pass to Lohaus, but UNLV is there to tip it away. Quickly they run it up the floor, kick it to the left, and the Running Rebels drain it to make the score, Iowa 66–65. Davis calls a time-out with 10:54 remaining on the clock and the Hawkeyes in disarray.

When play resumes, Iowa works the ball inside to Marble, he takes it up strong, but is unable to convert. Moments later, UNLV takes the lead on a three-pointer by Paddioa.

Iowa has been playing hard but has been unable to get the ball in the basket. UNLV has outscored the Hawkeyes 21–2 and now leads 68–66, with 10:07 remaining on the clock. For Iowa fans, it seems like time has slowed to a crawl as they watch their team struggle. The inbounds pass is almost intercepted by the Rebels, but mercifully goes out of bounds. It is still Iowa's ball, but the players are clearly rattled.

A scan of the two benches tells the story. On Iowa's side, every chair is filled, while the UNLV players and coaches are all on their feet. Momentum is a tough thing to stop. Marble, still playing hard, fakes and then takes it up, but he can't convert, and the Rebels are running again. Iowa fans breathe a sigh of relief when the shot is missed, and Gerry Wright pulls down the rebound.

At the other end, the shot bounces off the rim, then backboard, and UNLV knocks it out of bounds. Brad Lohaus gets the inbounds pass and sends it over to Moe. The ball is passed around until Moe gets it on the left side and puts up a three-pointer. It is short, and UNLV gets an easy rebound. Iowa looks tight.

The Hawkeyes may not be able to score, but they are still playing hard, getting back on defense, and Paddioa gets called for the charge. The basket is waved off—and Iowa ball.

B.J. slowly brings the ball across the mid-court as the clock winds under the 9-minute mark. It is anybody's game. Again, moving the ball back and forth around the outside until an easy pass seems to slide right through Lohaus' hands, and it is the Rebels' ball. UNLV passes the ball in, and Lohaus is almost immediately called for a foul while trying to trap.

Banks, showing great confidence, puts up an NBA three-pointer, and makes it look easy. B.J. takes matters into his own hands and quickly drives to the basket at the other end for a bucket. The first Iowa score since the Eisenhower administration. The Hawkeye fans are grumbling, there is frustration, but there is still hope, and yet, UNLV leads 71–68.

UNLV keeps firing up shots. They shoot, miss, Iowa tips the ball, but it ends up in Rebel hands. Another shot, again, nobody can find the handle, and UNLV gets it. They pass outside to Mark Wade, who holds up his hand to tell his teammates to get back under control. He starts to dribble. He passes underneath, and Iowa knocks the ball out, but Jarvis Basnight picks it up off the floor and banks in the bucket. UNLV leads 73–68.

Coach Davis calls a time-out.

It is a cliché, but this game is really a tale of two halves. In the first half, Iowa was shooting 72 percent from the field, while UNLV could only muster 38 percent. Now, the Hawkeyes are hitting at an anemic 29 percent, in part because of fine defensive play, while the Rebels are shooting 58 percent.

B.J takes the ball around the right side and puts it up. It's no good, and Ed Horton is called for the foul on the rebound. Jarvis Basnight will shoot the one-and-one for the Rebels. Basnight is a decent free throw shooter and makes 74 percent from the charity stripe during the season. In the tournament, however, he has stepped it up a notch, making 86 percent of his free throws. He makes the first, but misses the second, and Armon Gilliam is there for the rebound. He kicks it out, and once the ball is in Wade's hands, the Rebels start to burn a little clock. In the first half, they shot the ball before 15 seconds had wound from the shot clock, but now, with the lead, they play it smart and look for a good possession. They succeed when Gilliam hits a turnaround baseline jumper. UNLV leads 76–68 with 6:32 remaining.

Horton gets it into Marble, who goes up strong but can't get it to fall. He is fouled by Gerald Paddioa. Roy calmly steps to the line and makes them both, cutting the lead to six.

UNLV rushes to the other end, and Freddie Banks puts up a three but misses. Al Lorenzen times his jump perfectly and pulls down the board. He immediately passes it ahead, and Iowa is off and running. Gamble gets a good look, but it won't fall. UNLV takes it the other way.

The clock is down to 5:42, and Lorenzen fouls Gilliam as he gets the pass down low. Armon Gilliam makes them both to bring his scoring total for the game to 25.

Iowa works the ball around until Lorenzen takes it inside. He draws the Rebel defenders and dishes it off to Marble, who lays it in. UNLV 78–72. Iowa is still playing the full-court press, but UNLV has gotten comfortable working the ball up court. A long pass, out of Gilliam's reach, skips off his hands and out of bounds, Iowa ball.

At the other end, Gilliam goes for a steal on the B.J pass, but fouls. Iowa takes it out of bounds. One more foul, and they will be in the bonus. It was Gilliam's third of the night. The Hawkeyes get a lob pass into Gamble, and he scores. UNLV 78–74.

UNLV is still playing their up-tempo style, and Freddie Banks puts up a three-pointer, but misses, and Kevin Gamble battles for the rebound. He gets it. Everyone dashes to the other end. Gamble passes to B.J., who sees Marble under the basket. He throws a bullet pass, and Marble takes it up but is fouled by Armon Gilliam, his fourth. Roy makes one, and the score is UNLV 78–75 with 4:21 to play.

UNLV runs some clock and then finds Basnight under the glass; he puts it up and in. UNLV 80–75, and the clock shows 3:39.

Jarvis Basnight tries to steal the inbounds pass but fouls Gerry Wright. It is his fourth foul. Wright makes the first, but misses the second, and UNLV pulls down the board.

Wade gets the ball inside to Armon Gilliam who turns and fires—good. UNLV 82–76.

Iowa, down by six, looks for a quality shot, but the clock is ticking. At 2:40 left, Armstrong tries a three, but it is a little short. Wade comes away with the rebound.

Banks puts up a shot in the lane, he misses, and B.J. gets the rebound. Running to the other end, he dribbles the ball behind his back, to his left, and then takes it all the way to the bucket for two. UNLV 82– 78, with only 2:05 left in regulation.

UNLV, up by two possessions, is content to move the ball around the outside. 1:40 on the clock, and Wade pulls the ball out almost to center court. He sends the ball inside, but a diving Brad Lohaus comes up with a steal, and there is hope in all of Hawkeye land. It is short lived. The ball is stripped at the other end, and now UNLV has a new shot clock, with only 1:26 remaining.

Iowa fouls and calls time-out. Banks steps to the line. He's an 80 percent free throw shooter and has a chance to extend the lead to six. He misses the front end of the one-and-one, and Iowa has the ball.

UNLV switches to a zone. They want Iowa to shoot from outside, and with :34 seconds left, Gamble takes the trey. He makes it. UNLV 82–81.

Iowa is pressing, the clock ticks down, and UNLV is unable to get it across the time-line. Iowa ball, with 22 seconds remaining. UNLV, who has only lost one time all season, is in the fight of their lives against Iowa, who also occupies the number one ranking this year. The fans from both schools are cheering, but a lot of them are wringing their hands, too. This is why sport is great.

Coach Davis uses his last time-out.

Armstrong takes the inbounds pass and dribbles to his right. Gamble is near the top of the key, Lohaus is down low under the basket, and the clock reads 00:19. A lob pass to Lohaus is too strong, and it bangs off the backboard and out of bounds. UNLV ball with 00:14 seconds remaining, and Jerry Tarkanian calls his last time-out.

Iowa is able to foul, but it is Gary Graham who is shooting 94 percent, from the line, during the tournament. He dribbles and makes the first of his one-and-one. He rattles the second one home and UNLV leads 84–81. Iowa has 10 seconds remaining and zero time-outs.

Iowa brings it up quickly, and a B.J Armstrong pass is deflected out of bounds. Iowa ball with 6 seconds left. The ball is passed in and then over to Gamble, who is covered by two men. A three-point shot will send it to overtime. Gamble fires and … the Iowa season, a great season, comes to an end.

Forty

2012–Spring

A cold day in January, 2012. Roy is surrounded by quiet. He sees the basketball in the corner, picks it up, and slaps a strong hand against the leather. It is still the sweetest sound he knows. It has been two decades and counting since his sophomore year, and the mark of thirty wins stands. The friendships remain, and stories are told whenever they get together. Roy is thankful for that time in his life. He treasures the memories, and it is nice having his scoring record and the others remain on the books, but it isn't the best thing in his life. On the dresser sit the tickets for the February 4 Penn State game, where the old gang is going to get together and wax nostalgic one more time.

The recognition from the fans will be nice, seeing everyone will be wonderful, but it will all pale in comparison to the pride of sitting and watching the current Hawkeyes play. When his son, Roy Devyn Marble, # 4, runs up and down the court, he won't be Roy Marble from the thirty-win team so many years ago, he will be a dad and a fan. To Roy, there isn't anything better.

It starts and ends with being a fan.

00:00

About the Author

Brian D. Meeks met Roy Marble in early 2011 and they started talking about the season. Brian, the author of the Henry Wood Detective series, started reading about the team and thought it would be a good story. Roy, the all-time leading scorer for the Hawkeyes, had great stories about growing up in Flint, Michigan, and how he and his buddy, B.J. Armstrong would decide to go to Iowa, together. They both agreed it would make a good book.

The author can be found at his blog, http://ExtremelyAverage.com or on Twitter @ExtremelyAvg. His bio on Twitter sums him up well. " I have delusions of novelist, am obsessed with my blog, college football, and occasionally random acts of napping. I also Mock! Will follow cats & guinea pigs.

He is a graduate of Iowa State University and through the writing of this book has learned that the arch rival Hawkeyes are pretty good guys, too.